The
Something Shiney
Journey

Jennifer C. Tabora

THE SOMETHING SHINEY JOURNEY
From the Depths of Depression to a Life in Abundant Joy

ISBN: 9781735476100
Library of Congress Registration
The Something Shiney Journey

Category: Nonfiction > Body, Mind & Spirit > Inspiration & Personal Growth

Nonfiction > Family & Relationships > Love & Romance

Written By Jennifer C. Tabora > Jennifer Tabora

Email: SomethingShiney@outlook.com

Contributors: Kimberly Receveur, Michael R. Myers

Edited by Rachel Cox

Cover Photo: Michael R. Myers

CONTENTS

DEDICATION

To every person who has ever suffered in silence, been brokenhearted, and felt like giving up I dedicate this book to you that you may experience the same comfort that God, through Jesus Christ, has given me.
II Corinthians 1:3-5

The Something Shiney Journey

ACKNOWLEDGMENTS

To a very special person, Kimberly, you have given me the most valuable thing you own, your time. You have spent hours on this project, unselfishly given yourself over to the completion of this work, never once asking for anything in return. I want you to know it is through your devotion that I have learned the greatest lesson in my life which is, "you are the church" and we all have a chance to be the church in someone else's life. Thank you for being a living example and the backbone from which the church is built.

To my husband and children, thank you for allowing me the time I needed to finish this life-long dream. I would not have been able to do this without your love and support.

To my family and you know who you are, Thank you for the years we have spent together. You make life worth living and give me something great to look forward to everyday.

To all of those who have been a part of my journey. I want you to know God has a way of making the ordinary, extraordinary.

To the Church, I have learned so much from you and I look forward for what God has in store for each of us!

....come and see what God has done....

FOREWORD

I am a survivor from the back hills of North Carolina, who quit school in the eighth grade and was raised by an addict. It was addiction that dictated the conditions of my life, my heart, and my soul. I know at times you'll read this in first, second, and third person, but this is my story and often times that is exactly how I felt. I was different versions of myself sometimes experiencing life being fully present in the moment, but often times not. Of course this was my life before Him.

I want you to know that I did not grow up with God; I just knew this song that told me there was a man named Jesus who loved me. I suppose that is all I needed to know to experience a new life, a re-do, truth is I got a "start-over." The very thing I wanted as far back as I can remember.

I want you to know that it was God who took what seemed to be an unsurmountable task and made it as easy as stepping over the Colorado River.

Yes, the Colorado River the same river that is one thousand four hundred and fifty miles long and stretches more than five hundred feet wide. The same river I stepped over in the Southern Rocky Mountains ten thousand one hundred and eighty four miles above sea level; far away from where this journey started in the basement of my New Jersey home.

Why is this important? Because that is how big I thought my pain was. I was so consumed with who I wasn't that I couldn't see who I was created to be. I was so consumed by what I didn't have that I couldn't see what was right in front of me. I was so busy pretending to be what everyone else wanted me to be that I could not love myself for who I was.

I started this journey with a pain greater than the grandeur of the Colorado River. The "gorges" of my suffering altered every decision that I made. Until, I left it all behind to follow the One who said "Follow Me." I was as unsure of myself and everything that was happening to me as anyone might be. I didn't have confidence. I didn't have self-worth or value. I didn't even know what that was because I never had it. I questioned everything and yet, I still followed the still small voice that brought me comfort in the middle of my pain.

I had no idea where I was going or how I was going to get there, I just knew one thing. I knew His voice when He spoke. I was innocent enough to shut up and listen and His grace was loud enough to stop my screaming from the inside. He quieted my pain long enough for me to hear Him and follow His lead.

I was in the Rocky Mountains when I stepped over the very spot where the Colorado River begins. It was then that I realized it is God who can take the impossible, the unbearable, the intolerable, and make it small enough to overcome. He can make it small enough to step over, just like He did with the Colorado River. Everything starts somewhere and it started with me crying out to Him in the middle of my pain. When I stepped over that river, I also knew that pain would no longer rule over my life, my heart, or my soul. I knew it had found its rightful place in my past and it

could no longer consume my future.

I am only a witness to the magnitude of an amazing Father who

loves me so much that He could no longer stand by and watch my

suffering. A Savior who loved me so much the moment I cried out

to Him, He showed up. It was like He had been patiently waiting

for me my entire life. He stepped in quickly without hesitation,

even though I had spent years chasing every single fleeting

passion. I didn't happen in a church pew; it didn't happen with

someone banging down my door to share "the gospel." No one

stopping me in the stores with a message of "good news;" it was

just me crying out in my pain, hoping He would see me in my

suffering and save me from myself.

I want you to know He is no respecter of man or woman. I am not

special. I don't have a degree; I am not a biblical scholar. I do not

know His Word by heart nor can I recite scriptures verbatim. All

that I have is my testimony. So this book is my version of Jesus

Christ showing up in my life. He has feed me when I had nothing to eat. He has clothed me when there was no one there to take care of me. He never stopped loving me even when I couldn't love myself. He has been faithful even when I was faithless. He has kept His promises to me even when I have forgotten what they were. More than anything in the world, I just want you to know that what He has done for me He will do for you and that He loves you with an everlasting love. He will never leave you. He will never forsake you. He will be with you until the end of this world and He is not a man that He should tell lies.

I just have one more thing I want to add. As you read through my story, all I ask of you is to give God a chance. If nothing has worked in your life, if you have failed on every turn, if you are broken, if you feel less than this world, all I ask is that you Give God a Chance. I did and I promise you, you will not regret it.

If you do, it will not be my story, it will be yours, and it will be worth telling.

Chapter One:

I am Clean

It all started when I found myself drowning in the depths of my depression. I spent my twenties going through intensive medicated therapy to try and deal with what happened to me in my childhood. It helped me cope with everyday life but it never healed what was broken. This is where the journey begins. I had tried everything else, before I ever gave God a chance.

I always wondered why there was a place that yearns to be filled inside of me. I know that it is there because I can feel the emptiness; it screams to be heard, to be seen, to be loved. I have nothing. I am nothing and yet the world around me says there is nothing that I lack.

How difficult it is for them to see past what I show them. How simple it is to assume everything is okay. It's like second nature to judge the condition of one's heart by their exterior presentation. It is so effortless to be completely dependent on what is seen; believing in a truth that is riddled with perception, altered by experience, and deceived by broken hearts.

The truth is, I have learned how to compartmentalize my mind. I have a face for every situation and every person in my life. I pour myself out like an opened faucet to be consumed by their overwhelming need for control, but I know me; when the time comes, I will turn the faucet off. Then someone else will come along and drill a new whole inside my heart, consuming the living water they have found there. The cycle will repeat itself, time and time again, until there is nothing left but a dried, used up, old well, and I will find the end of myself in a season of drought and death.

On the outside, it looks like I have it all together but really I am just a chameleon. I adapt to my environment making it hard to decipher who or where I am. I am present but I fade easily into the background. Now, the doctors can label me and say I am bi-polar, borderline, or have some kind of identity disorder but I know who I am and I know where I came from.

I have an amazing ability to blend in. If I didn't know something, I just pretended like I did, until I convinced those around me of the same. I guess that is how I got and kept great jobs. Accomplishments made me feel good; I was proud to be able to financially take care of myself after growing up so poor.

The problem was the moments of "feeling good" were always temporal. It never lasted and I would find myself staring down the barrel of a loaded gun; full of buckshot memories that shattered any hope for a future free from pain and mental anguish. It was as if my childhood swallowed up my life; shadowing over me, robbing me of any sunshine or rays of hope.

Horrific images breaking through the surface of my reality would just show up out of nowhere, popping in and out of consciousness. Sometimes those images haunted me but sometimes they had the power to carry me away. Just like right now, as I sit here and write to you, I find myself getting lost inside of memories of me when I was eight; looking up at the sky singing to the clouds, "My gray skies will turn to blue someday." I can still hear the innocent desperate attempt to assure myself "it would all be okay." Then, other times, I would beg God to take me home. I would tell Him through my suffering, I didn't ask to be left alone, to be tossed aside, or abandoned. I must've cried rivers full of tears trying to convince Him I didn't belong here on this earth. I pleaded my case. He never came, but that didn't stop me from believing heaven was my only home and knowing He was the only One listening.

I guess that gave me some kind of hope to hold onto but, more often than not, hope felt like a distant cousin; it only visited once in a while and often appeared in short crescents of time. It was in those moments that my mind got to be little again. I would stare up at the clouds to find little treasures dancing across the tree tops tossed about by the winds.

Even as an adult, I found hope much like a child would, in the lady bugs that would land on me once in a while or the beauty of majestic butterfly wings. I could imagine riding their backs and flying away, disappearing into the sky, leaving this entire life behind.

"Hope" became a way of escape for me. It allowed me to live in a place that was ever changing. Every day I managed to find hope where ever I was. It didn't matter where I was left or who I got sent to because I was always looking up at what was above me. I would find myself drifting away into the skies shifting clouds, moving across the heavens, because they were always different. Not one day like the next, there was nothing like being caught up in a whirlwind of early morning sunrises. It was like the day's dawning pleased my soul as it promised me something new and filled me with hope for a better tomorrow. An expectation of anything greater than myself, offered me something to look forward to. It gave me a way of escape. I could leave my body behind even if it were only temporary.

I learned to survive, but it was heaven that helped me. The sky was above me and everything else was below me. At the same time, the skies had a weird way of grounding me because they were the only constant in my life; unlike people. It didn't matter how ugly it got outside, on the darkest, on the gloomiest, on the most overcast days, the skies never lied; they told me exactly how they felt. They were faithful like that. I knew when they would cry or when they would be full of sun-lit joy.

Unlike people, who could be happy one minute and angry the next. They could be here one minute and gone the next. So, as a child, empty promises became normal and I learned to cling to whoever was there. I was never too sure how long they would be around or how long I would be with them. I learned quickly, "hope in people" would always let me down, but the skies never did.

It's no surprise that after a while, I lost my childlike mind and hope seemed to escape me. Instead, I became a prisoner of people. It was never their fault but I watched them carefully. I found security in pleasing them. It was like a disguise. I mimicked them and became a perfect replication of what they were, "parroting" back exactly what they wanted in order to manipulate their love for me. In some areas of my life it worked. I was often promoted to supervisory type roles in my jobs, but in other areas it would become incredibly degrading and volatile.

I was so desperate to be something to someone that I would become mesmerized by those who said the words, "I love you." I would put them on a hill, raising their stature above my own, allowing them to dictate my feelings with an expectation that they would be my Prince Charming. I was always waiting for the one who was sent to save me; the one who would make me whole.

I had never felt that way before, whole, complete, as if nothing were missing. I had always felt a gaping hole, an empty part of me anxious to be filled; as if my entire person were an empty Kingdom waiting for a King. It is no surprise, no bolt from the blue, that I accepted anyone who stepped up to the throne and answered the desperate cries of a broken little girl, all grown up. Yes, that was me! I spent my life pleading to be loved. Answering the calls from anyone willing to be king over me and complete what was broken inside. It was me who chose to be fulfilled by the distorted desires of a life found in pleasing someone else. It was me who felt as though I wanted to crawl inside their skin and exist only in them.

The truth is, that was my goal. I wanted to be lost in a love that I could only fantasize about. I had no identity. I didn't know what love was. I had never felt it and any glimpse of what love could look like, was taken from me. My only recourse was to become everything they wanted me to be, but that always left me on the same lonely road. I would choose to lose myself in someone else, giving all of myself, including any form of who I thought I might be, only to end up resenting them for it.

The truth is, the only throne I served was a self-serving throne; a throne that was disguised as self-less, always laying down my wants and desires to become a servant to theirs; in hopes that my servitude would somehow gain what I could not even express I wanted. I had chained myself to servitude. A servitude bound by unrealistic expectations. I gave all of myself away expecting to be made whole, but it left me with hatred in my heart, not towards others, but towards myself. I served one god; the god of hatred. I spent my life worshiping at the thrones of depression, self-loathing, and hatred in complete solidarity to commit violence against myself. I hated me and there was nothing anyone could do to change that.

I could not stand the sight of myself. I scraped and clawed at my face. I spoke unspeakable things slashing my heart into a million pieces with my words. I didn't need anyone else's help. I was fully capable of hurting myself, of tightening the chains of self-obliteration. I was broken and all I could see was my brokenness. I was focused on my pain and nothing but my pain; it became my giant. It was my Goliath and against it, I was losing every time. I lost when I beat myself in the head with my fist. I lost when I spent hours contemplating my suicide and sometimes, trying it. I lost when I looked for any token of love, desperate for something, for anything, or anyone to bow to my need to be accepted. The truth is, I never felt worthy of love. Who could love someone like me?

My entire life screamed from the top of its lungs, "You are worthless, disposable, without value, no one could love you, not even your own mother." The truth is life chose me but I didn't choose it. I did not choose to be born in a family riddled with abuse and addiction. It was not my choice to be abandoned, neglected, and mistreated. It was not my fault that the one thing I was supposed to have and didn't get was love.

I was fashioned for pure love, not the kind that is consumed by self-gratification. I was created for unconditional love, not the kind that is skewed in a magnificent display of smoke and mirrors. I had an innate ability to understand the kind of love I had become accustomed to, was not the kind of love I was made for.

I knew what I wanted but instead I settled for any resemblance of love I could find. In a desperate attempt to be loved I answered "yes" to every ugly memory in my life. The echoes from the chaos I accepted from every action of every person screamed louder and louder into my consciousness. I could no longer drown out the voices that brought themselves into my reality; as I agreed to be obedient and become a slave to dysfunction I got what I asked for. I asked for a king; a king to reign over my heart and control me in exchange for the hope that I might find happiness. Instead, what I found, inside the heart of another, was the crushing sensation of unrequited love. The kind of love I wanted I could not find, but that never stopped the chronic desire for it. The craving for a pure unconditional love drove me into the arms of my own suffering.

I learned very quickly that love equaled pain and without pain there was no love. This created some sort of slanted longing from inside of me to torture, twist, and distort what love really is and it all started from being a child of addiction. I may not remember much from those days, but I clearly remember desperately wanting to be loved from a mother that chose her addiction over me every time. I wanted to be loved by the people that I lived with or was left with. I wanted to be loved by my aunts and uncles, my grandparents and cousins. I wanted to be loved by the only father I knew but was taken from. I wanted the kind of love that would "keep" me no matter what; the kind that doesn't leave. I wanted to be valued and treasured. I wanted to be loved innocently from a place of purity and not perversion, but what I wanted existed only in the desperate, deserted places hidden deep beneath the emptiness inside of me.

The desire for love was so great that without even realizing it, I had invited my abusers from my childhood into my bedroom daily. Every relationship was a reflection of a past I was desperately trying to run from. Instead, "I will love you if" became a way of life. I was so desperate to be loved that I recognized love through the distorted lenses of shattered hopes and whimsical dreams. I truly believed that without the presence of pain love was unattainable. I had to feel it, to be touched by it, I needed a sensory overload to reach beneath the pain I caused myself in order for me to experience it. I was broken and nothing I tried put me back together; no relationship, no therapy, no friendship, no amount of success, and no amount of pain. Nothing worked.

It was not until I was at the end of myself, when I felt like I had nothing left, that the opportunities to give God a chance came knocking at my door or should I say my shower door. It was the strangest thing, I wasn't expecting it, neither did I plan for it to happen, it just happened, and it all started with me feeling like my life was over or at least I wanted it to be.

There was nothing that could satisfy the depth of the loneliness inside of me. I opened the door to the shower as the steam cascaded out into the air. I stepped inside to reach for the faucet as my mind told me to make it hotter. I knew it could never get hot enough, but I turned the nozzle as far as it would go. I had no strength to fight them anymore, but the utterance from my mouth broke forth from the clutches of my lips, as these words escaped me: "take it from me, please, because, I don't want this life anymore." I held a razor blade in one hand as I cried out to God with the other. My words broke free from the prison inside my soul and I said to the Father of all creation, "If you are real, save me from myself!"

The shower never could touch or cleanse the depth of my sufferings. The hollowness from inside of me split out on that shower floor as I fell to my knees in full surrender to a Savior I never knew. In that moment, a Deity I once sang to as a small child showed up. His grace blanketed me because I was too weak to fight. Too weak for hatred, too weak for pain; but in my weakness He gave me strength; strength to face the truth. The truth about all the pain I had put myself through. Jesus not only heard me but He saw me there. He came and sat with me in that shower. It was Jesus who never shuddered at all of my ugly truths, but instead, He loved me there. It was Him who met me on the shower floor, right where I was, alone, empty, and hollow.

My soul bore the darkened truth of my past. It was a truth I could not hide from. It was the truth that stole my entire life and the very truth I tried so hard to run from. I felt as though He covered me with a blanket of His grace. Right there, surrounded by iridescent clouds of steam with the force of showered droplets beating down on my back, He found me.

He held me there as He showed me a memory from when I was twelve. My Mom had taken me for my first abortion. At the time, I had no idea the depth of pain it would cause me. I didn't know that on that same day, a gapping whole would be torn open inside of my soul. A whole that could never be filled by the hopes of finding love, because I had just lost the most natural form of unconditional love that was ever created. The love between a mother and her unborn child, my womb had become a tomb and I did not even understand what had just happened to me. I did not understand that this ripple in time would vibrate horizontal transverse waves throughout the next eighteen years of my life. I didn't know it would ruin the ability for me to feel loved because the one person in the universe who was supposed to protect me was relieved she had just destroyed part of me. But the truth is she didn't know either.

Between the heat and the water pounding on my back, I felt as if it cleansed every ounce of pain my soul had ever suffered. I cried as He gave me the greatest gift ever given to mankind. He gave me the gift of repentance, and with each breath, I confessed every abortion that came into my mind. My heart was so hard and I didn't even know why. I didn't know my pain, suffering, and self-hatred came from the death of my unborn children. I didn't know the choice I made actually stole self-value and worth from me. I didn't know with each death, I died a little more each time. I didn't know, until that moment, abortion caused me so much pain.

My mouth felt as though it didn't belong to me; its confessions bellowed out from the depths of my soul as I asked Him to forgive me for every single abortion I ever had. I watched every single painful memory of the death that I had caused go down that drain. Each and every tear was washed away and for the first time in my life, I actually felt clean.

As I stood to my feet, getting up from the shower floor, I felt like the weight of air; a thousand pounds lighter. The world had been lifted from my shoulders; my body as light as a feather. I stepped out to dry off and grabbed a towel to wrap around me. Time felt like it stood still as if caught inside of a trance in slow motion, I turned to leave and reality came flooding back. I watched my hand reach out to take hold of the bathroom doorknob and just as I did that, I understood, I was stepping back into the very situation I wanted to run from. My abuser, waiting on the other side of that door; I forgot I had brought him with me. I had brought the pain of my childhood with me and I chose to live with him every day.

The moments of abuse came flooding back. The three of us lined up on the couch as he paraded our mother out in front of us. We watched him twist and turn her wrist upwards behind her back and slammed her face into the wall. I wanted to cry but I knew I couldn't. I was not allowed to show him my weakness. He had trained us well as he described to us the color and smell of fresh blood. He pulled his gun out from the waist of his jeans and pointed it to her head. He told us the power behind a bullet held enough velocity to splatter her brains across the living room wall. All I could think of, my heart pounding in my throat, was "Please, God, no. He is hurting my mommy" and I was too small to make a difference too afraid to scream for help. I was frozen much like what I am right now.

As I walked out of the bathroom, I knew nothing in my life had changed but my whole world had changed. I stepped into the bedroom. The ashy stale smell of cigarettes saturated my lungs. The filth of my life was all around me. I couldn't instantly change the decisions that had brought me to this place. I couldn't snap my fingers and make my circumstances disappear, but I knew I would never again try to scrub away the dirtiness of my soul with soap and water because I had finally been made clean. No spot, no blemish, no stain, I wasn't tarnished or discolored. I felt the brilliance of His light illuminating the radiance of my soul. I felt as if I had been clothed in white with an oversized garment that dangled from every limb and whispered to every part of me that I Am Clean.

Chapter Two:
The Truth Shall Set Me Free

I closed my eyes and took a deep breath, just like I had done so many times before, as I walked across the bedroom floor. I did not want to disturb him. I had to quiet the excitement exploding inside of me. I swallowed what had just happened, like a knot inside my throat, I felt it all slide inside my belly.

Over the years, I had learned how to "steer" my relationship with my abuser, but all that I had learned became distorted and foreign to me. Something had instantly changed inside of me because I had just encountered real love; pure love, unconditional in all of its form, no expectations or disappointments, just love, accepting me as I am kind of love, unadulterated like I had never seen it before kind of love. I stepped out of that shower and into this bedroom and right away I knew how he treated me was a living contradiction to what I had just experienced. What I did not know was how to navigate this new truth.

A truth that reached every corner of my being, it touched every thought, and told me I was clean. This new truth had overcome generations of lies passed on from parent to child. It fought every

falsehood that I had been told; every plague over my life was

halted in its tracks. This was a truth I had never experienced, a

truth on steroids as if it had grown muscle overnight; strong

arming every fabrication of deceit into submission. This truth was

a truth that had conquered the win, victory was raising and the

winning consumed my heart.

This truth made me fall in love with a Savior I barely knew. This

truth was no longer a question; the question mark had been

removed and replaced by a period. "I Am Clean" went deeper than

my external skin. It bypassed my brain and everything I swore was

true and landed in the darkness of my soul illuminating a love that

I had never experienced. It was not based on performance or

manipulation. It was completely outside of any ability of my own

and it was more than I could have ever hoped to imagine.

However, this new truth, this new love, could not change the fact

that I was still very much right smack dab in the middle of a very

dirty situation. I had come to accept this victim / abuser lifestyle as my normal, but it contradicted everything that my soul had encountered in that shower. It wasn't something I wanted, but it was something familiar. This was my relationship, the very one I chose. I wouldn't wish it on my worst enemy, but it was what I knew and I found comfort in holding tight to it. There were no surprises. I knew what to expect.

What I didn't expect was to get the most devastating news of my life. I was not ready to deal with the death of my mother. She had passed away and I still needed her. I needed her to be normal. I needed her to be my mother. I was not ready to bury the hope of ever having a "normal" mother daughter relationship with her. The one person I loved from a distance. The one hope I still clung to was now gone and I had to face that, by choice, I stayed away. I stayed as far away as I possibly could, because it hurt too much to love her.

As a child, I knew my mother was always different. There was something special about her but also something very sad. Over the years, I had managed to separate the different personalities she had. I don't know that I loved them all, but I could tell the difference and always wondered if anyone else could. Patricia was the home-maker, PJ was the partier, and Pat was tough and had tough jobs; like construction, electrician, and soldier. Patty was the little girl, but she stayed hidden most of the time. When I was small I didn't really understand how to put her into words but I can articulate it now.

Every part of me believes that her addiction was somehow driven by her inability to cope with everyday life, but that is not an excuse. I will not excuse her from the decisions she made that hurt her children and destroyed her family, but I do forgive her. I understand her more now than I ever could have before. I can be honest by saying it is true it hurt me too much to be in relationship with my mother, but that did not change the desire to be loved by her. It took years to understand that she was my first encounter with love and it hurt to love her. It also hurt to be loved by her. I don't know if she ever encountered what love really looked like, but my guess is she had also learned that love equaled pain and that is what she passed on to us. I do not believe it was intentional but it was what she knew. She knew love equaled pain and every one of her relationships taught us just that.

It is not that I didn't try, but when I did, I got hurt. It was easier to stay away and not go back for more. I did everything I could to avoid pain. I did not want to feel and my mom made me feel every time I was near her. We could never have a regular conversation because they were always riddled with I'm sorry and please forgive me.

She made it difficult for me to speak with her. She always reflected on the past. A past she never let go of and never forgave herself for; even though I repeatedly told her to. We were a family of five; three girls and two boys. We all have very different stories of a pretty jacked up childhoods; from every form of sick abuse and neglect imaginable. For me, if I avoided my family then I also avoided having to think about a history I was trying to run from. It hurt too much to think about the family I once had. I didn't blame her but I did blame her addiction.

Even still, I wasn't prepared to say good-bye. I was still holding on to the hope that one day I could have a normal relationship with her. She was only forty-nine years old when she died. Her addiction finally caught up with her and the news of her passing had caught up to me. I fell to my knees and sobbed. I cried hysterically because I had lost my mother. I lost the mom I remembered as a child. The one that would sit me behind her bent knees on the couch and feed me butter pecan ice cream while she watched Soap Operas. The one who taught me the "Jesus loves me" song and laughed at my silliness, the one who hugged me so tightly that I thought I would surely burst and Yes, the one that made us all scrambled eggs on Sunday mornings and peanut butter balls at Christmas. There was a time when she was "normal" and so different from the way she spent the final twenty-five years of her life.

After getting the news of her death, I laid on the floor weeping and thought of her last words to me. She said, "I heard you are moving to New York; you know I am not going to see you again. So, I came to say Good-bye." It was so strange; she showed up like she always did, out of nowhere. I didn't even know how she knew where I lived.

After she left, I realized she stole my shoes. I laughed and thought that's just like her. I never thought of it again as I finished packing and moved to New York. Not until now. Now I ask myself how she could know what I could not even imagine.

We said good-bye that day but I didn't take her seriously. I never thought it was really going to be forever. If I would have known I would have asked her to stay longer. I would have held her tighter. I would have said I was sorry. I would have reminded her of the mother I remembered as a child, because she had replaced her memories with all the bad ones. She never could let them go. I wanted her to know that she was a good mom and that I knew she loved me. I wanted her to know that she was kind and she was not defined by her addiction. I wanted her to know that when I was small, her love shined so brightly that it blinded me from seeing her in her addiction.

I can't tell you how long I wept on that floor, but when I got up all I wanted to do was go back to North Carolina; the very place I had wanted to run from my entire life. It reminded me of the scene in *Forest Gump* when Jenny goes home and starts throwing rocks at the house she grew up in and, eventually, Forest has it torn down. I had done everything to put as much distance between me and those back hills as I possibly could have. For me, it was never really a specific place because I threw rocks at my entire existence.

 I had spent so much time running away and trying to forget about my past that in a blink of an eye, with one event, it all came back to me and I was instantly connected to the only other people in the world that could understand; my siblings. I wanted to get in my car and go as quickly as I could because in that moment nothing else mattered.

It didn't matter what my abuser wanted. He was always so excessive. He wanted me to fly there, then take a limo to the funeral, and then fly home. He wanted me to make a statement that screamed to an entire small town, "Look at me now." He wanted me to say, "I am better than you." He wanted to be in control of something that was completely out of his control. For the first time, I didn't care what he wanted, I just wanted to jump in my car and leave as quickly as I could and for the first time, in a long time, I did exactly what I wanted to do.

When I got the news about my mom, he had called a good friend of mine, so she was ready to drive back to North Carolina with me. I was so thankful I did not have to do it alone. I appreciated who she was in my life and how much she loved so freely. I often wondered what that felt like; if she ever felt lonely but silenced her pain. This time, I was simply grateful that someone cared for me enough to show up; to help me get through one of the hardest times in my life. She had an intuition about life that I lacked. She knew when to be there and when to bow out and let someone else take the lead.

I don't really remember much about that week. It was painful. I spent most of my time slipping in and out of my "little girl" mode. Mostly I stayed in the back ground and kept silent, watching in pain as the world turned around me. I wasn't really present. I was hiding and I was hurting. At one point my sister in law said to me, "Jennifer, you have changed so much, you hardly even wear make-up." At the time, I hadn't even thought about it. I just agreed with her because she was right.

So much had changed since we last saw each other. I remembered how I used to wear make-up as a mask because I hated myself so much. I would cry while looking at my reflection in the mirror. All I could see was my ugliness and all the things that happened to me. I would ball my hands into a fist and punch myself in the face until my anger subsided. Then I would get up, clean myself off, and put on my face. Afterwards, it made it easier to see my reflection in the mirror, it was an acceptable mask; a way of separating me from what I perceived my reality to be.

I made sure I put my mask on for the funeral. I was ready. I did not want to cry. I just wanted to get through it. I received a phone call from the mortician advising me to come early to see my mom before the wake started. I can remember walking through the funeral home. As I stepped through an entry way into another room, I saw my oldest brother and sister standing over her body. It was covered by a white sheet. My sister lifted the sheet to cover her shoulders as she looked up to see me standing in the door way. The delicate touch of her fingers had so much love in them and when her eyes met mine I could feel her sorrow, her pain, her tears, her loss because it was also my own.

You are never prepared to see someone you love in a lifeless body. She was a shell; not moving. I had never seen her so still. It became very apparent she was no longer there. Her loud personality was gone from this earth. Her voice was finally silenced. She could never again add or take away from this world and I wasn't prepared to see her like that. I had no choice but to let go of the hope that she would somehow be in my life one day and I wasn't ready.

I never made it to her side to stand next to my siblings, to look at her close up. I could only see the profile of her face and crazy hair. Her body had no life in it. It was so still. It scared me because even in my mother's addiction she was always so vibrant, loud, and full

of life. We sometimes still yell across department stores in

remembrance of her, but I couldn't go any further. The moment I

saw her, I gasped for air between my cries and the inescapable

truth that she was really gone. I ran as quickly as I could and

collapsed in the closest chair. I cried and repeated, "I can't see her.

I can't see her like that. I can't do it." My dad was there to comfort

me. He told me it was okay. I didn't have to see her. It was okay to

cry.

You have to understand, in the hardest of times of my life, my

daddy was always there. He just showed up when I needed him the

most. I mean, I didn't even know him until I was almost two and

got taken away from him at six, but it never failed. When I had no

one, he was there. He picked me up at eleven when my mom went

to prison and I had nowhere to go, he signed me out of some

mental institution my mom put me in, he showed up to bring me

home when I ran away. He was with me when I got married and

divorced. He is my earthly daddy and I know God sent him to me

as a heavenly gift. God knew I would need a dad just like him.

I could always be myself around my daddy. I never had to hide when he was near me. He was the only one in the whole world I felt safe with. He kept me and he loved me the way a father is supposed to love a child. He was forgiving, kind, and gentle. He was patient and seemed to have all the answers to my questions. I was grown now, in my thirties, and yet the little girl I kept hidden from the world always came out when I was with my daddy because she felt safe.

He was with me as I wrote my mother's eulogy. I must have asked him a bazillion questions about God. I don't remember the conversations much and can't really remember what I wrote. I know for sure, it definitely said something like, "our mom had given us wings to fly far away from this place." I am not sure what everyone else thought but I wanted all of them to know our mother, the black sheep, the cast out, the one who never felt good enough, was loved and cherished by her children.

My daddy was the one who actually read the eulogy. My tongue was gripped by grief. The smallest of utterance would cause me to cry inconsolably because I was burying the hope of having her in my life, which I held on to for twenty-five years.

When his reading came to an end, he looked up at each of my mother's children and said, "Your mother got her dying wish, which was that her children would be together again one day and here you are, all together, for the first time since you were separated as children. Now, don't let time separate you anymore." After her funeral we said our goodbyes and went back to life but it could never be life as we knew it. Something had changed. Everything had changed.

As I drove back to New Jersey, I swore I would never again lose my family. I promised myself and in a way I was promising my mom that I would not forget to stay in touch and do whatever I could to make sure we would never be separated again.

I can't remember much of what happened after arriving home. I just knew that New Jersey could never be the same, at least not for me. At some point, my abuser offered me a beautiful heart-shaped ring with scalloped diamond edges and I accepted. Soon after, I found out I was pregnant again. I knew I had to tell him, so I did. He had only one thing to say and that was he was not having a "half breed" baby. I knew I didn't want to do what we had always done before. I wanted our baby to live, so I explained to him what happened to me in the shower hoping he would agree to let our child live. I explained how I encountered the truth, a loving Savior, and a gift in the form of repentance but none of that mattered to him. The hope I had of saving our child was gone when he handed me the abortion pill and told me to take it.

It was so crazy; my mouth was on auto-pilot as I was listening to myself respond to him and I was shocked at the boldness of my tongue. I didn't even know where these words came from but I said, "I will take it because you are telling me to. I want you to know you hold full responsibility for this action because this is your decision. I do not want to have another abortion but I recognize you are the head of this house. Therefore, I'm going to take it but I know there will be consequences and I don't know what they are."

I took the pill and went to bed. A few hours later, it started. He never even woke up. He didn't care. It wasn't important and neither was I. I got up from bed and went to the bathroom. I started bleeding and crying because I knew what was happening. I felt the baby pass through the birth canal and into the toilet. I wanted to look but couldn't; I flushed the toilet and walked back into the room. Afterwards, I lay in bed and cried while he lay next to me. I cried for the death of another child. I cried because I flushed it down the toilet. I cried because it was wrong and I knew now what I didn't know before. I cried because God forgave me and I did it again. I thought to myself how could God still love me after this?

A few weeks later, I remember waking up in the middle of the night to the sweetest fragrance. It was like an orchestra of early morning kisses with overlapping aromatic cascades of citrus and floral smells playfully mixing all at once. I didn't want to go back to sleep. I didn't want to open my eyes. I didn't want it to end. I was afraid it would go away. I laid there, breathing deep breathes. Taking air into and expelling it from my lungs. I felt as though the very essence of my Father woke me up with the most beautiful aromas.

I believe He wanted me to know He was mindful of me and He would never forget me. He knew what I was thinking, He knew my struggles, He knew that I loved flowers and He used all of that to reach through my sorrow to touch my soul. The very place where my feelings had been hurt; I wanted to be good enough to have a child with, to share a life with, but I was not. God knew my heart because He knows me better than I know myself. I had no idea this would be the last time I would ever feel the kind of pain that says I am not good enough. Instead of leaving me in my sorrow for doing exactly what I knew God showed me was wrong, He chose to give me the most amazing bouquet of my life. The satisfying breath of relaxation and every beautiful smell ever created filling my room, refreshing my body, and strengthening every part of me cradled me back to sleep.

Later, that same morning, I found myself waking up to the putrid

smell of chain smoked cigarettes. For the moment, I had forgotten

that I lived with a furnace. I realized that my "Kingdom" started to

crumble and distaste towards "my king" had entered into my heart.

I literally could not find the aptitude to love him anymore. I knew

after what I had experienced in the bedroom that my God still

loved me, but I did not love him. A hatred began to grow inside of

my heart and I did not care about anything; especially him. The

switch had been flipped. The faucet had been turned off and he had

never experienced the kind of rebellion that was about to confront

every measure of his control.

After the will-full death of our last child, all I wanted to do was

run, but somehow, I knew what I really needed, was more of Jesus.

A war was raging inside of me and I began to hate men. Every

ounce of hatred stored up for twenty-nine years was seething just

beneath the surface. I know it sounds like the most untimely

moment but the first thing I did was buy myself a bible. I bought

the King James Version mostly because I was from "Bible Belt,

North Carolina," and had always heard it is the only true version of God's word.

At first, I read only the letters in red because I knew these were the words that Jesus actually spoke from his mouth. I skipped over everything else. I didn't want to know what another man had to say. I didn't want to hear from anyone else. Jesus was the only one I wanted to know about. In my life, so many men had been abusive to me. I couldn't trust anyone not even the black letters in the Word of God. I only wanted Jesus. I was angry and hurt and wanted to know if what had happened to me in that shower was real. I wanted to know if the smells that filled my bedroom were real. I wanted to know if God was real. If He had really showed up and if so why did I have to go through this again? Why did I have to face abortion again? Why did I have to bow to the desires of men? I hated men. I did not want to bow. I had seen my mother bow my entire life. Men were always the important ones while we were thrown away, sometimes, lucky enough to get leftovers. I did not want leftovers anymore, I did not want a hand-me-down Jesus, what I wanted was to know He was real. That Jesus is tangible, ever present in my time of need. So I read the red letters and they helped sometimes. I wasn't very consistent at first, just here and there when I needed to step outside of myself and my situation.

After my mom's death, my younger brother came to live with us and became a witness to all of my craziness. He was actually hired by my fiancé to do some construction work. Having my brother so close to me made me feel like I had a home. However, that didn't stop me from going a bit crazy after the death of our mom and the willful death of another child. I was determined to live my life the way I wanted. I would disappear, stay at my friend's house. I met a guy. I even had an abusive fling. I was a mess but somehow I managed to keep my work life intact. I had a mask for every version of myself. It worked long enough for me to get what I wanted and get out from under my fiancé's control by moving out.

It was New Year's Day when I left him. The same day my brother packed his things and went back to North Carolina. It wasn't the first time I wanted to leave or the first time I packed my bags to leave or the first time I threatened to leave but it was the first time

I actually left. I packed my car, gave him back his heart shaped ring and moved in with someone else.

At the time, he made it easy to leave him. I couldn't wait. I anticipated it. I hated him for what he did. I hated him for not loving me the way I needed to be loved. I hated him for knowing how to use me, how to manipulate me, and make me serve him. I hated him for feeding off of my pain so he could feel through me. I felt I had the right to blame him for every evil thing in my life, and, at that time, I felt he was the evil that hurt me and I no longer wanted his kind of love.

None of that stopped the measure of control he had over my life. I had changed my location but my heart was still the same. I had no idea how hard it could be to walk away from someone you have obeyed for years. Once, he convinced me to go with him to see a friend in upstate New York. On the way back he wanted to drop me off at my apartment. I knew there was no way I wanted him knowing where I lived. So, I told him to take me to my car. He showed me the knife he had in the seat between us. My body froze as if bolted in place and the memory of every measure he used to control me came flooding into my mind.

I remembered when I woke up to him dragging me out of bed, down the hall and down the basement stairs by my hair in order to "shut me up." I remembered the countless times he forced me to do unimaginable things to please him. I remembered how his desires were always more important than my value or worth. I remembered the threats of violence, the anger, the outburst, the choking, the weapons, and the tools. I remembered the relentless shame that followed from pleasing him and how it stole any measure of shine I had left to give to the world.

It angered me that he knew about some of the abuse I had suffered as child and he used it to his advantage. He knew about the memories that haunted me. The beatings, the abuse, it never went away. He knew my dreams were plagued by fear. He knew all about the night terrors I had. He knew and he still put a knife between the seats and a gun beneath him. Why would he show me that? What were his real intentions? I believe he knew that the moment he showed it to me fear would grip my soul and that is exactly what happened.

While sitting in his truck, his actions echoed a past I could not escape from but I waited for the moment that I could run. I would run from every evil word that escaped his lips that night. The fear of what was in him and the darkness of his eyes pierced through me with such intensity my heart-beat throbbed inside my ear drums. I moved my hand closer to the door and when the vehicle came to a stop, I jumped out and ran into the darkness. I didn't know exactly where I was. What I did know was the darkness wasn't scary. The coldness of the air wasn't scary. I found a sanctuary hiding behind trees until I knew he was gone. I called a friend to come pick me up and take me to my car.

It wasn't long after I left and moved into my own place that my brother returned from North Carolina to do more work for my ex-fiancé. I wanted to see my brother, so I convinced him to stay with me at my new apartment for the weekend. When he showed up he was surprised to meet the guy I moved in with. He wanted to know what was wrong with me and I couldn't answer him. When the weekend was over I agreed to drive my brother back to my ex's house in Manalapan. I wasn't expecting to stay. I had no intentions of returning to that house or of ever moving back in with the man I despised, but time has a way of wearing you down. After all, throughout the months of our separation there were lots of flowers, gifts, and one time he surprised me by showing up in North Carolina, when I was on a visit to see my son; who lived there with his father and step-mother. He actually helped me buy a vehicle but I made sure, he knew, there were no strings attached; silly me. He was tenacious; what he wanted he usually got, and, at the time, what he wanted was me.

So, when I arrived to drop my brother back off he asked me to come inside. I was hesitant at first but then agreed. My ex's mom greeted me and gave me a big hug. She told me how she missed me and encouraged me to tell her son the truth about everything and not to worry that everything would be okay.

After talking with her, I agreed the best thing to do was to be honest. So that is what I did. I told him I was in a relationship with someone else. He told me that it didn't matter all he wanted was for me to come back home. He loved me and we could work through anything. He was an amazing manipulator and he made me feel bad for what I was doing to our relationship. He took me back to the apartment. As I packed my things, he kept the man I was with in the kitchen. He handed him a knife and begged him to stab him, so he could get away with murder. It is unimaginable that even after all the craziness I would still come back.

I would spend the next five months in pure emotional and mental torture. After all, I left him, I was living with another man, and I was going to pay for the decisions I had made. The problem was it didn't matter what I did or didn't do; it would never be enough. I had to watch him burn himself with cigarettes repeatedly as he would tell me I caused him to do it because it was the only way he could deal with the pain. He encouraged me to burn or cut myself to show him how much I loved him and how much the relationship meant to me, but I knew it would never be enough.

The sexual exploitation and abuse became so intense I thought for sure he would eventually kill me. I was ashamed of what he had turned me into. I was fearful and afraid to leave him, now more than ever. You see, I was a "good" girl before but now I was bad. I was worth even less to him now because my "good" girl image had been destroyed and could never be repaired. I deserved to be treated like the piece of garbage I had become.

His control became even more intense. I had to account for every minute of every day. I had to unyieldingly prove I wasn't wasting time. If I wanted to go to the store, I would need to make a list of everything we needed in the house and map out all of the stores in the city. So I could identify the best, most quickest and effective route to get the job done. He said it was to make sure I had a plan and I used my time wisely.

If I wanted to jog at night, I had to prove I had done enough work around the property, and the house, as to not be wasteful with my energy. In his terms, "If I still had energy to jog at night I must not be working hard enough around the house." After all, why would I want to run around in circles? If I wanted to be like a dog, he could treat me like one. I had to answer his every call even if it was to light his cigarette that was sitting next to him. It didn't matter where I was or what I was doing, I had to constantly make myself available to him. The barrage of insults and name-calling was relentless. He had been doing it for years but the intensity had increased beyond measure and when someone tells you that you are stupid long enough, you believe them.

Since my return home, it didn't take long for me to be cut off from everyone I knew. I had to quit my job and stay with him nonstop, constantly by his side. I wasn't allowed to leave or do anything without permission. I was isolated with the exception of those who were in our home. I was desperate. I needed guidance and the bible I had purchased was confusing. I wanted to hear from God but the words in the King James Version just sounded poetic. I loved to read it and it seemed beautiful but I didn't understand what it was trying to tell me.

I was so lost. Then I remembered that someone told me to find a bible I understood. They advised me to go to the store and read a little of all the versions then pick the one I understood the most. So that's what I did. When my ex fiancé (current boyfriend) saw me reading the bible, he told me I could not make an educated decision to choose Jesus over other religions until I had studied all world religions. So, instead of studying all the religions, I hid from him while I read the bible. I read it in the basement and sometimes outside. I started reading it like a book, from beginning to end. I wanted to know more. I wanted Jesus to show me His Word was real and He was real.

At the same time, my boyfriend was becoming increasingly annoyed by me. He would play that song, by Guns N' Roses "I used to love her, but I had to kill, I had to put her six feet under" and tell me that is how he felt about me. He even brought a loaded gun into the bedroom and put it in his night stand next to us. He knew I struggled a lot with depression and at the time I believe I had difficulty with differentiating what was real and what was in my mind. The coping mechanisms I had learned, through years of medicated therapy, were drifting away into a space riddled with triggers.

My mind couldn't keep up with the bombardment of harassment day in and day out. I would find myself hiding and hitting myself in the head with my fist more frequent than ever. I didn't want to live this way anymore and I didn't have a way out. I could never escape him now. It was worse than it had ever been and I didn't see a light at the end of the tunnel. Nothing seemed to get better it just kept getting progressively worse.

There were some happy times, when he was away. I would get some relief because he worked in Washington D.C. and had to travel. When I reflect on it all now, I just can't believe he bought a gun and would leave me with it alone. I am fairly sure it would have been much easier for him if I would have successfully committed suicide. I think he knew that he left me with an answer, readily available, to my problems. He provided me with an option to end all the abuse in the bottom of his nightstand. It was not until what he knew became a very real moment for me that he almost got what he hoped for. I found myself sitting on the floor, staring

at the gun, lifting it to my head when suddenly someone started

banging on the door. Yelling, "Jennifer, are you okay?"

"Jennifer!" It was a familiar voice that snatched me out of a

moment in which my world would have ended.

It was my daddy, his familiar voice just seconds before I had

forgotten everything. I forgot how he stayed with me after Mikey

went back home again. I forgot how he was a silent support for me,

encouraging me each step of the way. I forgot he was the one who

told me to buy a bible I understood. I forgot how he stayed in the

basement and did the chores around the house for my ex fiancé,

who paid him.

Perhaps my abuser had implemented a plan to help him-self feel

secure in our relationship by using my family to keep me there

with him but, ultimately, the very tool he tried to use against me

was the very tool that helped me gain the strength I needed to

leave. I didn't know I would need a support network to get me out.

As a matter of fact, I wasn't even planning to leave. I wanted desperately to make this relationship work, but God had other plans.

As often as I could, I read. I read the bible every day, just like a book, and every day I found myself reading my bible more and more. Until one day on the back patio something changed inside of me and I haven't been the same since. My abuser must've been away or busy somewhere because he wasn't home. It was a beautiful summer day in Manalapan, New Jersey. I had been reading now since February and had gotten to Deuteronomy Chapter 30 verse 8, which said, "And You will again obey the voice of the LORD and follow all His commandments, I am giving you today."

Those were the first words that leaped from those pages and landed right smack dab in the middle of my heart. Simultaneously my soul leaped, my eyes were opened, the veil was lifted, and somehow I knew that the same strength Jesus had to carry Himself to the cross was the same strength I had living on the inside of me. Alive and well, full of power, complete strength; I jumped up, ran downstairs, and told my dad this amazing revelation and he responded with, "Well, yeah, of course it does." I said, "You knew this and didn't tell me?"

I didn't get the excitement I was expecting, so I had to call my best friend. I told her the news. I couldn't wait to share with her this amazing truth. This unveiling of God's Word and how it jumped off the pages and landed right smack dab in the middle of my heart. I couldn't wait to tell her that in the blink of an eye, my soul prospered and her only response to me was, "Of course, Jennifer, didn't you know that?" I couldn't contain my enthusiasm, and yet I also didn't understand how everybody knew this truth and didn't tell me.

I knew, from that moment forward, I wanted to tell everyone what God had told me. I wanted to scream it from the mountain tops, but I was still living in the valley. I wanted everyone to know they were strong and could do anything God asked them to. This truth had captivated my soul. This amazing truth had no ability to ever let me go. I could never again, no never, never, never, never again be the same; I could not un-know what I now knew, and what I knew told me that I had the strength to do whatever God asked me to living on the inside.

God had equipped me for the journey, packed my back pack for the trip. He told me to follow his "commandments," those He would give me today. At the time, I did not know the Ten Commandments so the interpretation of the word "commandment" meant whatever tasks or prompting He put inside my heart. He miraculously imparted the knowledge I needed to listen to His voice. Somehow I knew when it was Him speaking and all I had to do was to follow His guidance.

He simplified my journey and packed my bag with the truth that would help me arrive to the destination He would bring me to. This simple truth changed everything. It set me free from the bondage that had tied my soul to a lie. My faith grew wings when God equipped me with ears to hear the most amazing truth ever revealed to all of mankind. A truth that tells me, "The same strength Jesus used to carry himself to the cross, is alive and well, living on the inside of me!" I had finally been set free from the lie

that told me I was weak, insignificant, and without worth or value.

The truth is the Word of God became a "Living Word." It jumped

from the pages and landed inside my heart, telling me what I

needed to do and who I really was. Little did I know that truth

would spark a journey into a world where no bondage had the

ability to keep me. I would experience freedoms I never even knew

I needed. It would be the truth about myself that would finally set

me free.

The Something Shiney Journey

Chapter Three:

God Wins

I walked around for weeks awestruck from what I could not forget. His words continually echoed in my spirit. They would not let me go. Every thought, every moment, kept bringing me back to His words. I could not run from it or even ignore it, my heart wouldn't let me. His words repeating themselves over and over again, "the same strength Jesus used to carry Himself to the cross was the same strength I had living on the inside of me."

"He carried Himself." I kept thinking of the strength He must have had to "carry Himself." I mean, I knew of the Easter stories. I had been told of the death and resurrection of Christ, but I had never read it for myself. Until that day, I found scriptures in Isaiah 50 and 53. I found them in Matthew and remnants of his torture in Psalms 22, John 3, 1 Peter, Galatians and so many more.

I couldn't get away from this truth that continued to echo inside me. It pulled me further in and I continued to read. It was like the entire book pointed to Jesus and what He had done from the cross. It told a story about a redemptive God and I wanted to know more.

I needed to know for myself that this person who suffered and uttered not a word: the One who was crucified, but innocent was real.

I needed to know more about this Jesus; more about the One who died for all my sins, who died to heal me, who offered his cheek, for me, as they plucked the hairs from his beard. He accepted the mocking crown of thorns, for me, as it pierced His skin while they placed it on His head. He was beaten unrecognizably; to the point His flesh hung from His bone and He did that all for me. I didn't understand it and I am not even sure I agreed with it, but I knew it was true. It was Him who laid His life down for mine. It was Him who carried Himself to the cross, but I also knew that God had told me I had that same strength living inside of me. I knew with that kind of strength I could do anything. I could do whatever God would ask me to.

Around that same time the movie, "*The Passion of the Christ*" had been released. I can remember that I cried the entire time. The screen was mostly blurred by the tears which flooded my eyes. It reminded me of all that I had read. I kept watching and thinking that "He carried Himself" through all of that physical pain, how excruciating. I could see all that was happening on the outside of His tortured body but I wondered what was happening inside His soul. The rejection, the hatred, the pain of losing everyone you love including your Father. The pain of being wrongly accused and tortured for crimes you never committed. He was crucified, he asked God to take away the cup, that must have meant He didn't want to be crucified, but His obedience reverberated inside my heart.

The strength of His obedience outlasted the people who He poured His heart into; His very own disciples: the same ones who turned away from Him and scattered at the time of His greatest need and what about those who falsely accused Him? His heart must have broken into a million pieces when the same ones He once spoke to in the synagogues chained and crucified Him. And yet, the revelation that His strength was living on the inside of me seemed beyond my ability to comprehend. The same strength to be physically tortured and not be at fault, to stand firm on what God says, without thought of the cost; that strength was alive and well, living on the inside of me. I could hardly fathom the depth of that truth, but I was consumed by it.

I found myself reading the word, full of passion to know more. I was angry at my past, but I had found a truth that superseded all that I had ever gone through. I was in Deuteronomy, the fourth book in the bible, thirty chapters into the eighth verse, when He first spoke to me. "You will again obey the Lord and follow all his commands I am giving you today." It was those words that stayed with me and it took a while for me to find them.

It took a while because it was difficult for me to read for any length of time. I could barely sit down for fifteen minutes. I hardly ever watched movies because my mind never stopped turning long enough to catch my attention. My entire family refers to me as "the Something Shiny Queen" because it doesn't take much to distract me, but there was something different about this book. It captivated my heart. I couldn't put it down. I wanted to know more. I wanted to get close to Him. He spoke to me and I couldn't wait to hear what He had to say again.

I know there are some people that will read this and find it hard to believe, but I can only attest to what I have experienced. My Jesus had become personal; I knew it was Him because there was something different about my soul. It had been changed by an understanding I could not explain. An inner knowing that touched me by "Truth", and, not just any "Truth," the kind of truth full of grace and mercy, like I had never seen or heard of before.

A truth that revealed the condition of my heart like a mirror reflecting into the deepest parts of my soul, I could finally see "me." It wasn't until that day in the shower that I was able to reflect on my past and see clearly that there was something wrong with what "I" was doing. It was always about what somebody had done to me, but that day was different.

That was the day He changed my perspective. It didn't come in the form of judgment, it didn't come in the form of I told you so, it came in the form of Love. The most amazing encounter was with Him who clothed my nakedness in mercy as I held a razor blade in one hand and a cry out to God in the other as I said, "save me from myself."

As I sat on that shower room floor, I was given the most amazing gift ever given to all of humanity. It was repentance and that repentance changed me. It wasn't a have to. It wasn't a "check mark" or even a "to do." It was a gift that I didn't even know I needed. I had some questions about this God that I encountered in the shower, because I had never felt such freedom. It was crazy; my whole world had changed but there was no evidence of my world changing on the outside; it only existed on the inside where no one could see it but me.

Even though I had an incredible encounter, I was still desperate for more truth. I still had questions and I needed answers. It seemed like no matter what I did when I opened the bible only one question came to mind. All I wanted to know was if what I had encountered was real. I wondered if He was really real and did He really want to love me?

Although I didn't recognize it as Him, at first, the truth is He affirmed His love for me in little subtleties of daily life. He answered small prayers and encouraged me each step of the way. He continued to do that for me until I came to the point that I realized there was no doubt left; no questioning, no pondering, or deliberating over the reality of Christ in my life. It got to the point that I knew I had seen His mercies for myself. I had seen Him working in my life in a real and tangible way. I was convinced of this new reality of a Jesus who loved me.

He convinced me with little things like tuning my radio to a Christian station. I didn't even know they existed. So, in that moment I was presented with a choice and I chose not to ever change that radio station. I memorized it on that channel and left it there. It was Him who planted the seeds of desire to seek Him out more. It was Him who used people to guide me into a relationship with Him, to buy me a bible, invite me to church, and sometimes use perfect strangers to encourage me.

At this point, there was no changing my mind. I knew it was Him and I knew He used people. I knew that because of all that I had been experiencing first hand but I also knew that because the bible is full of people. Full of stories of disappointment, challenges, victories, heartbreak, and over comers; the message seems to be universal, Fear Not and Trust Me for I AM the Lord they God, who sees, who loves, and who redeems.

I had so many questions. How could I find the answers to all of them in the bible? How could this book change my life? I bombarded my dad with the magnitude of my curiosity; it was always easier for me to hear from someone else than to actually read. I remember my dad's first description of my God. He described God like the Father who puts you in a head-lock, gives you a noogie, and tells you "now go try again." My friend told me that God was like having your first cup of morning coffee with your best friend, but no one knew to tell me I had His strength.

73

My mind was still processing the fact that Jesus was alive and well, full of power, living and breathing inside of me. It was like a long awaited fresh glass of water that I could not get enough of. My spirit was parched. I could feel the flooding rains fill my soul drowning out all I thought I was not. It was as if God were only leaving behind what He created in me and got rid of all that He didn't. He told me who I was. He told me I was strong and I could do anything asked me to. He told me He accepted me as I am and that I would obey Him above all else because my strength comes from the one living on the inside of me, but I still wanted to be sure.

I wanted to be sure. I wanted more. I wanted Him to show me again, and again, and again. I wanted it to be continually tangible and undeniable. I didn't want it to ever fade like so many other memories. I didn't want to sing the Jesus loves me song full of pain and despair. I wanted to sing to him full of praise in awe of His amazing love for me. I just wanted more of Him and the bible was the only way I knew how to get it. I wanted to hear Him speak again. I wanted to know His word as if it were the flesh on my

body, the living marrow in my bone; like blood running through

my veins.

The more I read the more I felt as though He shared some intimate

part of Himself and made me privy to a personal relationship;

divinely invited into a small space meant for two. It was Him and I

and we could take on the world. I felt as though I had snuck

through the back door of some celestial temple and secretly found

a truth that had been sacredly written on the tablet of my heart

from the foundations of the earth before I ever knew who He was.

At the time, I had no idea this first encounter with His truth would

change my life forever, which is exactly what I was looking for. I

mean, the only reason I had this bible in my hand was because I

had tried everything and everyone else. I just wanted to be happy,

but no one could help me. Even though I was carrying around this

new hope that I had encountered, there were still many parts of me

that felt broken, like the sum of scattered puzzle pieces that had no home. I simply did not fit but I had an uncanny ability to make everyone else believe that I did.

And so the journey began with needing answers and longing to feel the purifying presence of a savior like Him. The interesting part was it all started with the end of me. You see, I died on the day He told me Jesus lived in me. I died to self-hatred. I died to worthlessness. I died to the ability to serve a king that was less than the one true King, alive and well, living on the inside of me.

I had no idea what his voice was supposed to sound like, but I had an innate ability to follow it. I had no idea the soft subtle promptings were the guiding steps I needed to walk out of a tumultuous situation. His voice never came down from Heaven with a bull horn yelling, "Jennifer, turn right," but they rose up from inside of me. I knew what to do from my gut and it wasn't instinct. It was more than that. There was a consciousness of my Creator, a confidence imparted to me that I had never experienced before; in perfect chorus with a protection that covered me in my inability to hide what was happening on the inside of me.

The problem was what was happening on the inside of me was not "in chorus" with the environment I was living in. This became very evident on a day I was being forced to listen to another lashing from my abuser. The wounds he could inflict with his words cut deep and I had been held captive by it for years, but not this time. This day, it was different, because the more he spoke the more my eyes were opened, the more my ears heard clearly. I no longer heard his destructive words, instead I heard the manipulation that fed his egotistical demand for control. When I confronted him with it, he became full of rage. As I sat there, a witness to his barrage of male chest-beating, I am man hear me roar, craziness, I knew in my heart to never tell him what God was showing me. I put my head down and apologized; luckily, it defused the escalation of his wrath.

In those months, after my return, it was hell. I used a journal to express the ups and downs of my daily life. It was part of my therapy and I really enjoyed it. It allowed me to express the deepest parts of my struggles and insecurities in a safe way. Until, of course, my abuser found it. He found an entry I had made of a

list of good and bad things that had happened in one day. The bad

listed every fowl name he called me. Every moment he spoke

down to me and made me feel less than. Every violent gesture he

made towards me. It spoke of when he kicked me out of the car, in

the middle of nowhere, and made me walk for miles before he

returned to get me. I said nothing, when I got back in the car.

However, later I wrote in my journal of how I knew he wanted to

control me and have me be completely dependent on him.

It told of how his aggression made me withdraw and how I could

never show him what I was feeling. The good list spoke of the

times he held me when we went to sleep and how much I enjoyed

it. It told of how we got to skip the self-harming part of our

evening routine. It was always a goodnight when there were no

burns or cuts involved.

I had no idea my journal would make my abuser angry. It made

him angry because I spoke about secret things, things I wasn't

supposed to talk about or confront him with. He used my safe place to respond to me, but his only response spoke volumes. He invaded the only privacy I had, without cause or reason; he stole from me once again. As I read the words he wrote, it destroyed little pieces of remnant feelings left lying around waiting for some kind of redemption. I am talking about the very feelings I had for him; little by little, he was the destroyer of my hope for real, tangible reconciliation between the two of us.

His written entries had robbed all that was left inside of me. My heart broken as I read his words and thought to myself, I have no way out. No way to escape his measure of madness. I picked up my pen and wrote for the last time in my journal. It was the only thing that came to mind. It was the only thing I had left to say.

At the time I did not know, the final words I wrote that day were the finality of my future. They rose up from the depth of every tear I had ever cried. It was so simple. At the time I did not understand the fullness of what I had written, but I did understand the comfort it brought to my soul. It was only two words; they were definite and strong, and made a full and complete sentence. God Wins!

I do not know if my abuser ever read that journal again. What I do know is I left it open, with those final words beaming from the pages. Soon after that happened, we had a long conversation about how he would feel privileged if God chose to use him. He spoke of his grandiose ideals of leadership while being king over God's army and all I could think of was how strange it was to hear him speak of a God he didn't know. The same God he refused to let me study or talk about.

Over a period of a few weeks, I felt like God was prompting me to put a few things away when I did laundry. I listened and would take my favorite shirts or jeans, fold them, and set them inside a bag in the basement. I wasn't really sure why I was doing it, other than it must mean I would be going somewhere. In those weeks, nothing else was said. I had no other direction. No other revelations. So I continued doing what He asked me to.

The summer was going by so slowly. There seemed to be battles ragging between my abuser and me, over the simplest things. Like me wanting to take my son to Wal-Mart turning into an all-night discussion, with final permission being given the following day at 9:00AM; after being held hostage in the room the entire night before.

I knew, at some point, I would have to take my son home. He stayed with me every summer and I loved my time with him, but it didn't feel like I was packing for that trip. It felt like I was being lead to pack only my favorite things; my favorite jeans and t-shirts. At the time, I didn't question God, I just did it. I mean so far, everything He showed me happened exactly how he showed it to me. God had prepared my heart to trust Him, but I had no idea what was really in store for me.

While this was happening, my dad, who had come for the summer, was planning a fishing trip for us. We would celebrate my son, TJ's, birthday, who would be turning twelve soon. His plan was for us three to go to Wildwood, New Jersey. To the place we called, "The Mermaid Stomping grounds"; this was his cousin's house. It was his Aunt Mickey's house before she passed away. He would tell us crazy stories about her. He told us how she always had a seat and a plate for Jesus at her dinner table, and no one was allowed to sit in it. Once she called my dad and told him the hurricane had been good to her that year. When my dad asked her how, she said, the insurance man gave her a $10,000 check and told her not to use it for a pool. She agreed and proceeded to put in a pool. She told my dad, "I never even thought of that before he suggested it. Shoot, I'm eighty-six years old. If they ask, I'll just tell them the insurance man told me to do it." I had never been there before but I was so happy to get out of the house and away from the craziness.

It took about three hours to get there. It was beautiful. It was a cute little house off of the bay of the Jersey shore. It was built like a boat house made out of stone. The light switches were high up on the wall because the house flooded every year and every year, Aunt Mickey got a check.

The "Mermaid Stomping Grounds" was rich in love, and kindness. They were a colorful bunch with boldness in their character. The women in this place were strong in personality, full of life and laughter. I was so happy they were sharing their richness because I had felt so poor; poor in spirit. They lifted me with their Irish songs; singing along with acoustic guitars. Life was beautiful, sitting around a table with lights strung, crisscrossing against the night sky. I thought I had died and gone to heaven as I inhaled what living must really feel like. For the first time in a long time it felt as though my soul smiled.

In that moment, I was confronted with the truth. I had not been living; I had been surviving and then the phone rang. My cousin got up to answer it and called out my name, "Jennifer, it's for you." My heart sank and the essence of this magical moment dissipated with a phone call from him, my abuser. I didn't want to answer the phone but I did. I got up and walked around the back side of the house. It was a little dark back there but my cousin said it was closer if I went that way. As I passed through the darkness, a rickety old white fence gate caught my eye. It was covered in the over growth of neglect. They hadn't touched that pier since the last hurricane two years earlier. I could've sworn I heard the words "follow me" rise up from the pit of my stomach or should I say from the bottom of my soul.

I hurried to get the phone. His voice harsh, hard, sharp and pressing; he told me I had to drive back to the house that night and that I could return in the morning for the fishing trip because the boat wasn't leaving until 6AM. All I could think was how I was going to leave right now and be back by six in the morning. His house was three hours away and it was already past nine.

It was craziness, but how could I expect anything less than that from him. I hung the phone up and walked around the back of the house. Again, my eyes were drawn like magnets to that rickety old gate. I heard, "follow Me." I didn't think much of it at first. I just shrugged and kept on walking.

I got back to the table but I didn't want to say goodbye yet. I was falling in love with these people and their expression of living. I felt like I could breathe for the first time and I loved sharing the same air with them. This place was magical. I took deep breathes and laughed with them. I listened to them sing and let my soul continue to smile for just a bit longer before the phone rang again.

I stood up and told them it was probably for me and that I would get it. Their voices faded into the back-ground as the weight of what he was about to say pierced my thoughts like an anxious chokehold tightening around my throat. I couldn't swallow, but my eyes were again drawn to that rickety old gate and I heard, "Follow Me."

Instead, I hurried inside to answer the phone. I could hear the weight of his anger on the other line, the breadth of his rage being controlled by the manipulation in his tongue. His composed attempt to lure me into obedience by controlling me with fear had little resolve, because I had not left yet. His failure could be heard in the irritation of his voice and I could tell he needed to know he had power over me. So, I told him I was saying good-bye and would be leaving now.

After our conversation, I had come to a conclusion; I had no choice but to say good-bye. I didn't want to make things any worse than they already were. I hung up the phone as I prepared my heart to tell them I had to leave. I didn't want to tell TJ and my dad I would be back in the morning, or say goodbye to the mermaids. I wanted to stay, but I couldn't see how that was possible. My heart was breaking, full of sorrow, troubled by the thought of going back. I didn't want to go.

As I turned to walk around the back side of the house, I heard, very clearly, "FOLLOW ME." I looked up at that rickety old gate and thought, in there? You want me to go inside of there? I heard again, "Follow Me." I thought to myself, that's scary; what about spiders? There was only one response; "Follow Me." The entire time I was arguing with myself about going inside of that gate my feet wouldn't stop moving towards it. I tried to rationalize the fact that nobody had been back there for years and the only words that came back to me were, "FOLLOW ME."

I couldn't deny it, He was speaking again. My feet kept moving forward, until, my heart caught up with them, and then nothing was going to stop me from following Him. I walked towards the gate and lifted the latch to open it. I kept my eyes closed and stepped inside. A few steps forward and I realized I was standing on an old, broken-down pier. There were holes in it and it was barely sturdy enough to walk on. All I could think of was, "though I walk through the valley of death, I shall not fear." I didn't know that scripture but probably heard it somewhere before. It was all I knew and God used it. I repeated that verse as I zigzagged across that pier, dodging over-grown sea-weeds or whatever else grows in the back bay of the Jersey shore. As I got further down the pier it began to open up and became wider and wider. The further I went, the sturdier it got until I reached the end.

It opened wide up and the moon was so bright it looked like noon day. I really didn't know what to do. So I laid face down on that pier and said, "Okay God, here I am. I "Followed You" out here, now what?" I know this sounds crazy, but I felt as though I was being covered, clothed by the wings of some strengthening angel, I laid there with my eyes closed. I took deep breathes as if I was breathing in the fullness of my God, my Jesus, the One who I just met. I can't remember how long I was out there but it had to be a while. I laid there beneath the moon at the end of that pier and God held me. He loved me in that place. He strengthened our bond and told me I could trust Him, that He was a loving God. It was not really in words but I could feel Him there with me. My face down, the moon high and His abundant grace fell over me again and again and again.

Reassurance, fortitude, power, but mostly love; I felt His love for me. It was tangible. Somehow, my soul was touched by it and, once again, I would never be the same. My faith strengthened, and as I lay there, I began to see pictures play out like a movie show in my mind. I saw myself get up, go to the phone, and say to my abuser, if he wanted me home tonight, it would only be to pack my things and leave. Otherwise, I would see him tomorrow. I wasn't sure what God was showing me but I knew it was coming from Him.

Out of the darkness, behind the over growth, I could hear my dad

calling my name, "Jennifer." I wanted so badly to say, "God is

speaking to me, leave me alone. I am not ready to get up yet." But

I didn't. Instead I said, "I'm right here, I'll be there in a minute."

As I got up from that pier and stood to my feet, my knees began to

tremble. I was too scared to talk back to my abuser. I had been

controlled by him for more than six years; molded to be obedient

and not defiant. I told God I was scared to speak to him that way. I

had questions, like how was he going to respond and why did God

leave that part out?

I thought maybe I needed more time with God, so He could show

me what was going to happen afterwards, and then my dad called

my name again and I knew it was time.

It was time for me to do what God had showed me to do, but that

didn't stop the questions from bombarding my mind. As I traced

my steps back to that rickety old gate, I continued to ask questions;

like, what if my abuser agrees for me to come home to pack and

leave. Where would I go? I wasn't ready to say that to him. As I continued to put one foot in front of the other, I realized my thoughts began to bow to the vision that played inside my mind.

I told God, I had never talked back to him, but because He showed me in a vision what I would say, I would say exactly what God showed me. I expected the worst; my heart pounding in my chest, my knees shaky, barely able to stand, I walked back inside the house and picked up the phone. I dialed the number and waited for him to answer. I said, "If you want me home tonight, it will be to only pack my things and leave." I held my breath as I waited for his response. For a moment, he was quiet. Then he said, "It's okay, you can stay the night, I'll see you tomorrow."

I couldn't believe it. Why did I not hear anger in his voice? Had I just conquered a lion? I was in awe of this amazing God. The One who speaks and I listen; the One who knows more than I could ever possibly know; the One who held me at the end of that pier and who heard my heart when I said I wasn't ready to leave; the One who gave me what I asked for. He is surely, the One who cares for me.

I couldn't believe it. I really did have the same strength as Jesus. I had been persecuted by this man for so long and without cause. I had loved him and laid my life down for him. I did everything he asked me to do without question and yet he was my accuser. He accused me of being insolent, disrespectful, stupid, and disobedient. He was my giant; the lion that prowled the earth, sent to devour me, to destroy all that was good inside of me. Yet, my God saw fit to use me to shut the lion's mouth, to destroy the giant that came to destroy me and He did it with a vision.

Make no mistake. He used me. He asked me to carry myself to the phone and I obeyed. I can't explain with words the strength I needed to do that. I can only say that strength, that same strength that Jesus used to carry Himself to the cross was living on the inside of me and I tapped into it that day.

God taught me the most valuable lesson I could ever learn; which is, there is no giant bigger than Him. No Kingdom that can conquer

His Kingdom. No enemy that can defeat Him. No lion whose mouth He can't shut and no "man" greater than Him.

He is the GOD that Wins!

The Something Shiney Journey

Chapter Four:

A Way of Escape

We returned from Wildwood, New Jersey, on July seventeenth. I felt as though I were on top of the world. I had conquered the raging lion that had conquered me for so long. It was hard to hide the confidence of my faith. It had wings and wanted so desperately to fly which made the difficulty of hiding what God was revealing to me, nearly impossible. It had become the "elephant in the room."

The change was exceedingly visible. I felt as though it was happening at a pace I was having difficulty keeping up with. My mouth was becoming bigger than my ability to control it. The little girl hiding inside of me, the one who hid from any measure of confrontation was growing up. She was learning how to use her own voice and be heard, but this was happening beneath the surface where no one could see it, only me.

There was one problem; I couldn't stop holding my head a little higher and it seemed as though my presence infuriated every grain of my abuser's being. My eyes were no longer fixated on my feet. I started to make eye contact, but not intentionally. I wasn't trying to be offensive or provoking, but it was as if my abuser could smell the goodness living on the inside me and it enraged him. One thing was made very clear, my abuser had one nerve left and I was on it.

I knew I was not the same, because, how he felt didn't matter anymore. I could no longer mold myself into the image he wanted me to be; that encounter on the dock changed me. I could not be subservient to his every want, need, and desire anymore. It no longer mattered to me if he was satisfied with who I was or how I was behaving. I no longer needed his approval. I had an encounter with the One who approves of me. The One who loves me just the way I am and for the first time in my life, I was satisfied. I was satisfied with myself. I had a glimpse of God's love for me and it touched all the broken pieces. I didn't have the power to put my head down because it wouldn't work, my redeemer lives and He is the holder of my head. The reasons for fading into the background or into someone else were gone. I simply was not and could not be the same.

I did, however, continued to do my very best as to not inflame his violent tendencies and avoid as much conflict as possible. Mostly, I just kept myself busy. There was always something to wash. It was one the one thing I knew God was still asking me to do, so I continued to put a few things away in a bag in the basement. I loved it because it made me feel connected to an invisible but very present and personal God.

There was this one time, when I was looking for things that needed to be washed, that I went to my closet and that is where I saw them. The pants, my eyeballs glued to them, were still wrapped in plastic from the dry cleaners. I thought to myself, how am I going to get these past him? I have to walk right by my abuser to get to the basement, but that didn't stop me from plucking the black silk Swarovski Crystal diamond-encrusted buttoned slacks from my closet. They were beautiful and fit perfectly. I wanted to pack them so bad, but as I held them in my hand, I felt a question rise up into my consciousness, asking me, "Are they worth it?" and for a moment I thought, yes. Until the question changed in essence, this time, there was urgency to the question that I had not notice before.

"Are they worth him finding out what 'I AM' asking you to do?"

That changed everything; my heart was pounding in my chest as if

my abuser was privy to this private conversation going on inside

my head. I put them back just as quickly as I had taken them down.

I knew my abuser didn't know the conversation going on inside

my brain but my mind had been trained by him. I was scared to

hide anything from him because to me he knew everything. As

crazy as it may sound, he would have noticed if I had packed those

slacks. He kept me under lock and key; which included all of my

personal identity papers. I was lucky to still have my driver's

license. Throughout the years, he made sure I knew who he was

and what he had available to him. He would tell me things about

myself that I had forgotten. I think he did that to instill fear in me

so that I felt as though I couldn't get away from him. He made

sure to show to me how easy it was for him to find information on

any one, at any time, in any place.

He boasted about his position, the information he was privy to, and

authority he had with the United States Marshal Service. He told me about his access to top secret information and used his position to scare me. The truth is, I had no reason to believe anything less than what he demonstrated proof of. The evidence spoke for itself.

There was only one thing that he was not privy to and that was the conversations that were happening on the inside of me. I guess to some that sounds a little bit crazy and, believe me, there were times I questioned my sanity. No matter what I was thinking or going through it was God who never failed me. He would show me things and then I would actually watch them happen. It was God who was building my faith precept upon precept, step by step. Most of the time it was small things; things that no one noticed but me.

He was teaching me the sound of His voice. He wanted me to hear clearly, recognize Him when He spoke, and answer Him when He called. All I had to do was let Him be the guide, as I was learning, that God could do with ease what I couldn't do with all my effort, using every measure of strength I had. So I continued, little by little, only packing what would go unnoticed. I still wasn't sure where I was going or why I was packing. At one point, I thought to myself maybe I am going to Florida to visit my oldest sister. I didn't really get to spend much time with her after the funeral. She had to fly out quickly.

Time couldn't go by fast enough for me. I just kept putting one foot in front of the other every moment of every day, waiting, but not really sure what I was waiting for. There were some hard nights; nights that he kept me up until morning with antidotes of self-harm. I watched him burn, cut, and torture himself in hopes of controlling me. The animosity contaminating his heart was intelligently articulated in a barrage of verbal lashings. I could endure them, I had been trained by them, but life is not hopeful when you are helpless.

In those moments I could do nothing more but endure them, waiting patiently for the change or for some other direction. During those times, I thought of how some people say emotional abuse is worse than physical abuse, but, experiencing both, I think it accomplishes the same thing; it comes, it steals, it kills, and it destroys. I was tired and I wasn't sure what I was going through was normal. All I kept asking myself was the same the question, what was normal anyway and who defines it?

My mind would wonder off into places where I contemplated the normality of life and took into consideration our relationship. It seemed as if the only two things this life and this relationship had in common were shame and embarrassment. I would think about him touching me and all I wanted to do was run, but I could not do that again. I couldn't leave again and return because I wasn't sure I would survive another stunt like that. I just kept hoping that it would get better. It never occurred to me that there was a different answer.

It didn't occur to me until the answer came and it came all of the sudden. I remember the day so clearly. I made him lunch and he threw it in the trash. Expressing to me how pathetic I was and how nothing I did was good enough. I took the trash can from the bedroom and emptied it into the garbage in the kitchen. When I looked up, all I could see was the basement door. It leads to a place where I had found sanctuary before. It was dark and I could be alone. I needed to be alone with God. I needed to feel His love for me one more time. I needed to be strengthened to be able to continue living like this. In that moment, I no longer cared about what was normal; all I wanted was to be with the One who made me feel loved and that was the "new normal" I cared about.

I laid flat, my face to the concrete floor, buried in my hands. I cried out, once more, "Oh God, help me! I can't do this anymore. I am tired. I want to give up; I can't do it. Help me!"

Suddenly, I had another vision, like a movie playing out in my mind. I saw myself going up the stairs, down the hallway, and into our room. I saw myself telling him I wanted to leave to take my dad and TJ back home. I knew that it was earlier than I would normally take TJ home but that I just wanted things to get back to normal with him. I wanted it to be just the two of us.

I was scared, but I knew God was with me; He had walked me through something very similar just a week ago. I could do this again. I could do this with God. I was nervous but by now my faith had fortitude. I got up and did exactly what I had seen myself do in the vision. Once again, God didn't show me what my abuser's response would be but I knew I didn't need to know his response. I just needed to listen and do what God had showed me to do.

I got to the room and it poured out of me, word for word, without any effort and he couldn't have been any happier with my decision. As quickly as I could, I let TJ and my dad know we were leaving New Jersey and going to North Carolina. They needed to pack their bags as quickly as possible because we would be leaving in one hour. I didn't know why it was so important for me to leave as quickly as we did but I knew we had to.

My bag in the basement was mostly packed so all I needed was to get a few things from the room. I would be gone for seven days and staying at my brother house. He was okay with that. He had built some kind of trust up with Mikey and knowing where we were going must have given him some level of comfort.

I didn't have all the details but I knew we were not coming back. I told my dad but didn't tell my son, TJ. I just made sure he got all of his belongings. I grabbed my pictures, my bag, and remembered my jewelry. I ran back upstairs to get a few pieces from my jewelry box. He laughed saying, "What are you doing taking all your jewelry, are you not coming back?"

For one second, I lost my breath, before I knew it my mouth uttered the words, "Of course, I am coming back. I just like to wear my jewelry." He asked me to come close to him. My heart sank. As I got closer, I noticed he was looking into cruises online. He said, "I am planning a cruise for you and I when you get back." I said, "That's great. I can't wait to go with you." But inside, I knew I never wanted to see him again. He turned away and continued looking at cruises. I walked out the door, down the hallway, and back to the basement.

My duffle bag was so heavy it took me and my dad to carry it to the car, and we tried to act as normal as possible, loading it into the hatchback of my Jeep. My heart was pounding. It felt as though it was coming out of my chest. I had no idea where I was going; I just knew I was leaving. I was heading back to North Carolina where my family was, but there was still the impending feeling of doom, lurking just beneath the surface.

On that trip, we stopped in Wildwood to say goodbye to the girls and the Mermaid Stomping grounds. We went to the beach. The sand is gray there. I am not sure why I never noticed the color before. The water was cold but that didn't stop TJ from diving in. As I stood next to my dad, looking out over the ocean, I exhaled and said, "I can't believe I made it out, without any problems. It went so smooth. I am amazed at my Jesus." I was a little confused because I knew to lie was a sin. "Thou shall not bare false witness." That was a ten commandment sin. In my mind, one of the big ones, but, the truth is only God knows what is lurking inside of a man's heart. I had no idea at the exact time God showed me to go upstairs to ask to leave was the exact time he was looking into buying a cruise for us; to be alone together. My mind was still reeling to try and understand this God that I didn't really know but trusted with my life.

I asked myself on that beach if it could really be God asking me to lie to someone I supposedly loved. In that instant, my dad looked at me. He said, "I've been debating whether or not to tell you something." And, of course, I encouraged him to go ahead and tell me. He continued by saying he had been praying about my situation and didn't understand everything when he first got to New Jersey. To him, everything appeared to be okay until one night he got up to use the bathroom at around two AM. He said he overheard us talking in the bedroom and said it wasn't good. So he went back to bed and woke up again a few hours later to go to the bathroom. He heard the same conversation being repeated again and again. He said, "I heard him call you stupid ten times in just a few minutes." He told me he was sorry I had to go through that.

He told me how hard it was to stand by silently and let God work this out inside me, but he knew it had to be my choice or it wasn't going to work. He was a silent worker, dedicated in prayer, patiently waiting for God to transform my heart. In the end, he asked God if there was any hope and before he could finish saying the word God put in his heart to get me out of there. He said God

had given him a vision. He was reading a newspaper about my

murder and that I had been killed by strangulation. As soon as I

heard him say that, I fell to my knees and wept. I had never told

anyone what he did to me behind closed doors, but I knew that is

exactly how he would have killed me. I never said a word; I just

knew what he was saying was true and I cried.

We stopped on the Chesapeake Bay Bridge and went fishing. TJ

was the only one who caught anything but we all had fun trying. It

was nice to be out from under the pressure of pleasing someone

else while juggling my desire to make sure my son had a good time

with me. We didn't see each other but once a month, holidays, and

summers. So it was important for me to love him the only way I

knew how and that was to make sure he had anything he wanted

and that we had fun. I loved seeing him smile; it lit up the entire

room, especially my heart. He was my happy place and here we

were together.

On our way to North Carolina, my dad and I decided the safest thing for me to do was to travel across country to give it time between me leaving and him accepting that I would not be coming back. There needed to be distance between us. Otherwise, he could just show up and manipulate me into returning and it wouldn't be because I wanted to; it would be because I felt like I had to.

I mean, I knew I was not alone, but I was still vulnerable to his influence. I had not yet broken the pattern of abuse that I had become accustomed to with him. It wouldn't take much to convince me to return even though there was nothing in me that wanted to be with him. It wasn't love. It was a type of addiction. I had been desperate for him to love me for so long that any evidence that he might love me had the potential to imprison me once again. I had to do what I knew God was asking me to do, and I knew there would be a time that I would never speak to him again but the time had not yet come.

God had already cleared a path for me to follow and there was nothing more that I wanted more than to follow where He was leading me. God had restored my relationship with my family and with my father, the one who made me feel safe. He had prepared my heart to walk away from everything that I had known for the last six years. He asked me to trust Him and to let go of everything I had found superficial security in and take only one bag with me. He equipped me with the faith I would need to see this through. He transformed my heart by telling me that His love was more than enough. He forgave me, even for my repetitive sins. There was no doubt I knew something had changed inside of me. I had hope for a future. I trusted that He had a plan even though I didn't.

As the days passed, there was always one question in my mind: Is it time yet Lord? I felt more and more uneasy with each call, but I trusted God that I would know when and what to say when the time came. The truth was, I wanted desperately to tell him. I wanted to never have to speak to him again. To never have to answer another phone call or entrapping question from him. I was ready but it still wasn't time.

Until, it was. The phone rang, I answered, and he asked what I was doing? My heart beat got a little faster and then he said, "Why did you not tell me that you changed the address for your unemployment check to Wildwood, New Jersey?" In that moment, I knew this was it.

I told him I did not want him to know that I was not coming back. I would not ever be coming back and if there was anything he wanted to say, to say it now, because this would be the last time we would ever have any contact. He said a lot of things. He demanded I stay put that he would be flying there to pick me up immediately. He said he would give me the world. Even if what I wanted was a goat on a rope, he would give it to me. I stayed quite mostly. I wanted him to say his peace because I did not have anything left to say. I waited patiently for him to finish. When he did, I said good-bye and hung up the phone. I knew I would never again have to answer to him. I had just said my final good-bye. Somehow, I knew this time it was different. There was finality to what just happened.

I had my dad listening in on the conversation; having him with me, even though he said nothing, gave me strength to say what I had to. My dad was a bit taken back by the callousness of his words and narcissistic attitude towards me, but he knew what he heard probably meant we needed to leave right away.

We had talked about the trip we would take together across country. It was a good plan to get some miles between what happened to me in New Jersey and my future. He made it sound exciting, like a once in a lifetime adventure. I was ready. I had felt caged inside of a bar-less cell for years; caged by the scarcity of self-worth and value, but everything was different now. I couldn't wait for us to get on the road but I wanted TJ, my son, to come with us. I wasn't sure if his dad would have let him. I mean we had history. We were always good to each other and respected one another as parents and friends but taking TJ across country was another story. Not to mention, I think maybe TJ was ready to go home.

There were so many emotions as we packed the Jeep and got ready to leave. I said good-bye to my little man, TJ; I knew I would miss him. I remember my brother telling me to be safe and he would handle whatever showed up at his door. I took a deep breath and let them know I would be getting rid of my phone but would call as soon as I could get another one.

Every part of me was anxious. Every fiber of my body couldn't leave fast enough; fear of my abuser showing up had a grip on my sanity. It was difficult for me to keep it all together but my dad kept me calm. He could bring laughter into any situation. It was his super power; something that came natural to him. He had a knack for making life happy and fancy free. All the hard stuff just seemed easier when he was around. To my dad, life was a big comedy show and he made sure to point out the humor in it. Surely, he is and has always been God sent. Sent to help me walk through the hard stuff and bring laughter into what could have been a bitter soul.

We finished our good-byes, but none of it seemed real until we started the engine. I felt the vibration between my fingers as I held onto the stirring wheel and backed out of my brother's driveway. As I put the jeep in gear, I knew God was with me, that He was right smack dab in the middle of this mess and He was the one working it all out for my good. I can verbalize that now but then it just showed up in the excitement of the moment. My dad in the jeep with me meant I was not alone and God had prepared his heart and mine for the journey that was ahead of us. I had no idea where we were going but I knew it was going to be okay.

It was going to be okay because my God, the God of the Universe had provided a way of escape. Do you know what the word escape means? It means to break free of confinement or control. I was free! I was finally free! I could no longer be controlled by the demands of another. My prison walls had collapsed; I was free! No longer confined by the lies I had been told, I was finally free! Perfectly, imperfect, Free to be me!

.

Chapter Five:

The Mountain Top

We started out on our journey across country, leaving everything behind; one bag in tow and nothing but a blank slate on the horizon. The canvas of my soul was clean and rich with expectation. I was ready. Ready for the artistry of a magnificent God to fill every empty space with vibrant colors that defined what was happening on the inside of me. I was anxious to shine brightly so the world would know how great my Jesus really is, but mostly I was quiet.

My eyes had been opened but my mouth remained shut. There were no words to describe what was happening in me. My mind was silenced by the magnitude of His love. I was in awe of a magnificent God who saved me and who was reconciling the pain that had brought so much chaos into my life. I had felt empty for years; the land of my heart was parched. The ground was cracked and hard but the roaring rapids of God's truth had brought rivers into the dry places of my soul.

I was thankful that my dad was with me on this journey. We were getting closer to the Great Smoky Mountains of North Carolina, heading for the Blue Ridge Parkway, when we stopped to switch places at a gas station. I was grateful my dad wanted to drive. I think he knew I just needed to relax and absorb all that was happening.

We rolled the windows down, put the air conditioner on high and let the music fill the air as we cruised through the oldest mountain range on earth. The beauty of the lush green canopy blanketed every angle in sight. The blue mist that looked like clouds settling between the peaks and valleys on the ridge made me remember I always wanted to taste a cloud. How silly. How simple. So I put my head out the window, opened my mouth and stuck my tongue out. We drove right throu gh that cotton ball like mist, my mouth wide open, and the little girl inside of me smiled. A certain satisfaction overtook me as I thought to myself, "mission accomplished, I did it!" I finally tasted a cloud. It was like nothing, just air on my tongue, but to me, it meant the world.

Driving through those mountains I remembered how I always

loved the wind. The way it filled my hair and tossed it around

made me feel free; as if I were flying like a bird. I closed my eyes

and drifted back into a time when I was small; riding in the

backseat of my Mom's car through the hills of North Carolina.

Some of my favorite memories were of leaving the city and

heading to those old winding roads. Back then it was normal to

drive a vehicle without air conditioning. I can remember the

smoldering heat rising up inside of our car, but as soon as we hit

the hills, the coolness of the air would fill the car and bring great

relief; to a bunch of grumbling kids, who were too hot to get along

with one another. The memory of putting my hand out of the

window, allowing the wind to push it up and down; while, I

enjoyed the coolness between my fingers under the shade of those

old winding roads was still with me, even now. I had not forgotten

all that was good.

I can still see my Mom's radiant smile, as if frozen in time, she

would turn around to look at me from the front seat; young,

beautiful, and full of life. Just then, I decided to put my hand out of the window and allowed myself the privilege of enjoying that memory all over again. The moment was amazing. Right there, on top of Laurel Creek Loop, as we left the scenic route of the Great Smoky Mountains. Reprieve filled my soul with gratitude as I exhaled and let the heartbroken little girl fly into the wind and dance on the memory that filled her heart with joy.

I said goodbye to the home the Cherokees called "the place of blue smoke." I knew I would never again experience what these mountains allowed me to take away from them. There was a peace that settled inside of me much like the way the blue mist settled between its peaks. The waterfalls cascading through the rearview window, I felt as though the Great Smokey Mountains had shared with me one of its greatest secrets; harmony. A place where God's glorious acts move with one accord in a synchronized display of its beauty.

There was something amazing about driving through the wilderness that had been tamed by the hand of man; not in its fullest but just enough to expose God's great grandeur. I will never forget the lookout points displaying valleys of crisscrossing hills

that took on the appearance of hearts lapped on top of one another.

As I stared at those hearts, created by ridges and shadows, I

understood what man can give me is temporary, diamonds aren't

always forever, but God's love is eternal and what He had in store

for me was greater than I could ever hope to dare to imagine.

The cross over between the Great Smoky Mountains and the

Appalachian Trail onto the Blue Ridge Parkway into Tennessee

was breath taking. I spent most of the time absorbing the beauty

that surrounded me, until it got dark. Then my dad and I would talk

until I feel asleep. We talked about what I went through in New

Jersey. We talked about my whole life. There was finally someone

that I could tell all the ugly details that I kept secret. It was hard to

confess some of the things I told him just because I had not even

allowed myself to believe it was real. By talking about it, it

released the power it had over me. The light had been turned on in

the middle of the darkness and I told him everything. For the first

time I had no shame. I knew there was nothing I needed to hide

because I was with someone who had proven to me that he would never hurt me. He was my dad and my only safe place in the entire world. He drove all night as I slept.

In the early morning, when it was still dark outside, my dad got us on a straight away where we wouldn't be turning for a few hours, so he could get some rest. We passed through Missouri and into Kansas. Kansas seemed to go on forever. By the time my dad woke up, we were both in need of some coffee and he was ready to drive. There was nothing as far as the eye could see. I thought to myself, "Where in the world are we going to find coffee?" I mean, I had gotten accustomed to my New Jersey brew. It was the strong stuff but I would be happy with anything at this point. I didn't even finish the thought when all of the sudden I could see a tiny, little shiny yellow tin building on the side of the road with painted letters stretched from the ground to the roof saying, "COFFEE." I glanced over at my dad with an expression of "really" across my face, while, utter glee filled my heart.

I couldn't believe it. Everything that happened felt like it was mapped out by God. As if He was always one step in front of us.

We pulled in, and my dad took the time to clean himself up. He brushed his teeth with bottled water out by the jeep; while, I went inside. There was a book laid out on the counter with signatures in it. I asked what it was for. The lady at the counter told me that whoever passes through here signs this book. It was full of signatures. I flipped through the pages and read all the names. I was always fascinated by things like this. They made me feel a connection to the world around me. I appreciated having shared the same ground that was beneath my feet with them. So I signed it to; it was something I could share with them without any strings attached. I found it amazing that our paths had all crossed at this same point among the fields in the state of Kansas. I had something in common with every single person in that book which was we shared a small measure of restoration in the form of a nice hot cup of Joe.

As I came outside with our coffee, I noticed a piece of paper blowing in the wind. It blew against my shoe and got stuck there. I leaned down to pick it up and when I read it, I realized it was a short letter for someone who was deaf. It was one of those letters that asked for help but there was no one around. It reminded me of

the days when I once had a dream of being an interpreter for the

deaf. I worked at the North Carolina School for the death for

several years, but I managed to destroy the hopes of those dreams

with my divorce from TJ's dad. My ex's parents worked there and

I had packed up and left their son while he was shipped overseas

by the military. I remember telling him I wanted to go with him but

he said it was best I didn't. Looking back, I think I was trying to

tell him not to leave me. Although no one knew it, not even me, I

wasn't strong enough to handle the separation emotionally.

Unintentionally, I saw his absence as abandonment. I was still

young and had yet to deal with anything from my childhood.

Basically, I saw it as "out of sight, out of mind."

I stood there staring at that paper and I realized I needed to ask him

to forgive me for everything I had done. I had made choices that

destroyed my home, my family, and everything that I said I cared

about at that time in my life. As I held the paper in my hand, I

became astutely aware that everything and everyone mattered to

God. I knew He saw every person, every tear, every heart break, and He wanted to heal the broken places that were caused by my

hand and it would be Him that would use me to do it. Even though

I had no idea how, I just believed, I expected that God would show

me. So I kept it. I kept the note. I put it in the glove box as we got

inside the jeep and back on the road.

The road was vast and empty as far as the eye could see. So, I

talked my dad into going down one of the many dirt roads to do a

bit of exploration. It was hot outside, but not like the heat I was

accustomed to. I was use to stepping outside and feeling like I had

just stepped into a sauna, but not here. It was dry as a bone,

parched like a dehydrated landscape, burnt to a crisp, awaiting the

waters of official pardon. I looked up to see that my jeep was

registering 104 degrees outside. As we pulled over and came to a

stop I couldn't wait to open the door. When I stepped on to the dirt

road, a cloud of dust billowed around my shoe like powder does

from a baby's diaper. The wind lifted it into the air and swooped

across my face. I don't know why but I loved it. It felt like the

desert but with an expectant heart. It was as if the land knew it

would only be barren for a little while. I had never felt heat like that before. I made my dad take a picture of me in the middle of

that dirt road. It reminded me that though my heart was once dry

and hard, it wouldn't be like that forever. I was going to see God

do amazing things, impossible things. I got back into the jeep and

as we headed back to the main road I noticed the hills. They were

small hills that were vast and touched the horizon. The hills

seemed to bounce off of one another, back and forth across the

landscape; just like I would draw them when I was little. Until, that

moment, I didn't even realize they did that in real life.

It made me think that God must be bigger than the imagination of a

five year old little girl coloring on blank pages. He was sharing

with me the beauty that I would be seeing right now. Even though I

had never seen it before, He was demonstrating to me that He did

not live inside the constraints of time. To God my past and my

present were one; all the things that happened between right now

in this moment and then, were blended together in a beautiful

display of grace. I didn't have to tell Him the things I saw or the

pain I felt. He was sharing with me that He was there. He saw

every tear that I cried as I colored those hills in shades of vibrant green. The memory of the pain that I suffered came alive and was painted across the plains of Kansas. My mind became one with the reality of what was and the truth of a God who always loved me, who always saw me, who never forgot me, and kept me this whole time. It changed something inside of me to know I was never alone.

The road ahead of us seemed long and went on forever. At times my dad and I were quiet and other times we talked about my Mom and what she was like before she became an addict. My dad even told me about the first time he met me. I was almost two and he had a coke in his hand. Apparently, I wanted some. So he gave it to me; my little arm could barely reach the bottom of the bottle as I grabbed it, put it to my mouth, and tilted back my head, as far as I could go, to drink it. My dad also told me about the first time he learned I could speak. He said I was a tiny little thing. I was sick and he was taking me to Womack Hospital on the Fort Bragg Army base. He said I sat on the middle of the console in his car and talked the whole way there and the whole way home. I enjoyed listening to all the stories my dad shared with me. It was nice being reminded of the good stuff.

It was also therapeutic to talk so openly about everything to someone I knew loved me unconditionally, but I don't think it was only for me. I think our conversations brought some closure and understanding to my dad also. I can only imagine the choices he had to make, to stay away, in hopes it would cause us less pain and suffering. I am sure it wasn't easy. I know it wasn't for me. I was only six when we first got separated, then I was back with my dad at eleven when my Mom went to prison and I had nowhere to go. When he picked me up, it felt strange at first. Not because I didn't know him, but because, at that point, he had been gone for almost half my life. I wasn't sure how to respond or what to say, so I was quiet. It didn't take long for him to make me laugh and the laughter made me feel like I was home again. He explained I would be rejoining his family with his new wife and my younger brother and sister who I hadn't seen since I left. It didn't work out at first. I had so much pent up anger and they had no idea what I had been through.

I spent most of my teen years back and forth between the times my Mom was out of prison and living with my dad. Until, of course, I got married at sixteen. My dad signed me over at the courthouse and my Mom waived a white t-shirt from her jail cell in the window ten stories above us. I guess she wanted me to know she was there with me. I had lost touch with everyone after my divorce at twenty-one. I spent a couple of years making bad decisions before I left North Carolina to be with the man I now refer to as "my abuser." I was with him for six long years. It was my Mom's death that changed all of that. In a sense she is the one who reunited us. She finished what she started. It was because of her, we all were separated and it was because of her, we were all together again.

And here I was, thirty years old and back again with my daddy; on a road trip across country. The openness of the roads unlocked the hardness in my heart. I had no idea, all these years, I had been under construction. The hurt and pain was much like the asphalt we were driving on, created by those who built it, but beneath our tires was more than asphalt. There was land ready for the plowing; preparing our hearts like farmers do when winter is over and spring has come. The driving was putting the winter of my life behind me and spring was on its way. I wondered what it would be like to break through the hardness inside of me; the parts of me that no one sees.

My hand to the plow looked a lot like the freedom I was finding in sharing so openly with my dad. There is something remarkable about having the freedom to speak; it allowed the flood gates of stored up emotion to be released, and I think that happened on both sides. He didn't say anything but I could tell. Like I said, my dad had a knack for making the heavy stuff seem light. I guess God knew I needed a class clown for the difficult parts of my journey. There was no doubt he helped me focus on the good stuff while God was busy preparing the soil of my soul.

It was a distraction much like the layers of mountains coming up on the horizon; they were bountiful and their beauty could not be missed. The stunning display of mountainous grandeur captivated my eyes. I guess I could've missed it if we simply drove by, but I knew there were exquisite splendor, awe and glory, hidden between those magnificent white covered peaks. It was only a matter of time before I got to experience them for myself. What secrets could they hold? Was there something more to what I was seeing, something greater than what could be seen?

As we got closer, I began to think of the valleys in my life. How could I find mountains among them; were they there; had I gotten stuck somewhere along the way? Where were the peaks? What treasures did those valleys really hold? I wondered why these old mountains created such questions in my mind. And what were they stirring up inside of me?

We stopped at a hotel in Denver, Colorado, just below those peaks that had formed so many questions in my heart. I think we both needed a hot shower and some where we could enjoy real food. We had been on the road for days; munching on granola bars, stopping for hot cups of coffee, and occasionally enjoying wash-up-and-go pit stops. It was both exciting and exhausting.

We checked into our hotel, took showers, and walked across the street for dinner. There were water puddles on the ground which meant it must've rained while we were inside of our hotel room. I loved puddles. It reminded me of all the times I played out in the rain. It was one of the only things I loved to do as a child.

The streets in North Carolina would become like tiny rivers. There was no one to stop me, no one watching out for me, so I would stand at the door, watching for lightning, and run for the street as soon as the thunder stopped. It didn't matter what I was wearing, or what I was doing. I had one care and that was to get wet, kick my feet through the raging waters, hold my head back, open my mouth, and let the droplets of rain fall on my tongue. Those are the times I felt refreshed, made a new, like God Himself was giving me a bath.

I can remember the sun seemed to always come out from behind the clouds right before the rain would stop. My sister would always say the same thing. She would tell me that if it rained when the sun was out it meant that God was crying happy tears. Her words made me wonder what happy tears felt like. Ever since then, I never forgot about God's happy tears. The thought of them was always with me waiting on the days the sun would shine and the clouds would release His cries.

The puddles beneath my feet were a reminder that I must have missed the opportunity to catch God in action. Nonetheless, that didn't stop me from having an overwhelming desire to stomp in the puddles, but instead I listened to the reasoning in my head; I had just showered, I had on clean clothes and my good shoes; not to mention, we were going out to dinner. The feeling passed quickly with the onset of an entourage of "should not's." I had missed the opportunity to "live" but I hadn't realized that yet, so I stepped over the puddles instead.

It seemed no matter where we went or what we were doing every step took me somewhere else in time. Just like this restaurant. It reminded me of "The Ponderosa," which was the first steak house and buffet that I had ever been to. I used to go there when I lived in

Plattsburgh, New York, still married to TJ's dad. Even though I had never seen these places before in my life, this trip across country had become more like a trip down memory lane.

My dad and I ate until we couldn't eat anymore. We had our coffee afterwards and headed for the hotel. It was dark by now and we knew we wanted to get an early start in the morning. It didn't take long after our heads hit the pillows to fall asleep. The morning came quickly. My dad had already stepped out to get us coffee. As I laid there in bed, I noticed that there was a peace and tranquility about the sun rising through the window. As I sat up, I realized the peace and tranquility was deeper than daybreak; it felt as though there was light dawning on the inside of me. I had no idea what God had in store for the day ahead of us but I couldn't wait to get up and start packing our bags; the air was thick with anticipation.

The mountains were before us and our past behind us; not only my past but Dad's past too. After all, he had only been sober for about three years and I couldn't help but feel like this trip was not just for me. I mean I knew my dad was here for me. He came because I needed him but I also knew he was having his own encounter with God. His own private conversations as he was witnessing God's handiwork; not only in my life but also in his own.

We loaded the jeep and headed for the Rocky Mountains. My dad broke out in song, singing, "Rocky Mountain High." He bellowed out his own version consisting of the lyrics he remembered, "He left yesterday behind him, you might say he was born again, I've seen it raining fire from the sky, where you can talk to God and listen for His reply, Rocky Mountain High." I had never really listened to that song before, but it truly felt appropriate as the Jeep began ascending up onto the mountainside, beneath the canopy of trees.

The first stop was at the base of the mountain. I was so happy my dad pulled over. I got out of the Jeep. It was as if the river was calling my name in the subtle whispers of water rolling over the rocks. I had no idea it would take me back to "The Place." The place I would go when I was little, when I was being hurt, I had a safe place; it kept me there in my mind. It was a field of rolling grass that tickled the palms of my hands as I walked towards the

willow tree and the running stream beneath it. There were only

ladybugs and butterflies as I remembered my feet could actually

feel the coldness of the water between my toes. The rocks beneath

the water were all vibrant colors dancing across the pallet of my

eyes. I think Jesus would take me there so that He could inhabit my

senses with good. He protected me from the reality of what was

happening to my body, but that did not stop the fact that my

physical senses had been distorted. My innocence taken by a thief

hiding in the shadows of darkness; intimacy had been forever

distorted. My taste disturbed by indecent liberties. I had been

touched by dead hands. My eyes violated by things no child should

see. My hearing echoed the memories of words that would have

been better left unsaid. But instead, in the worst of it, in the thick

of the storm, I remembered, I had the feeling of soft grass beneath

my feet; the smell of flowers in my nose, the touch of butterflies on

my fingertips, and the taste of cool water stimulating my senses.

My mind preoccupied with the remembrance of a past long

forgotten, I bent down over the stream to touch the coolness of the water. I looked at it for a moment, turned to my dad, to ask if it was fresh mountain water. He said, "Yeah, it is from the melt offs from the snow." I didn't think about anything else. I drank it from the palm of my hand and when I did, it was like drinking from the water that flowed through memories of all the moments Jesus saved me as a little girl. The coldness of my heart was melting, like the snow from the mountaintops, my hatred washed away as I drank from the river on that day.

I stood and looked up the mountain, as far as the riverbed would let me. There was something bigger on the horizon, something more I was supposed to be seeing. "What is it," I wondered, "a pilgrimage of self-discovery?" I was being divinely inspired to go further, to dive deeper, and to see what I had never seen before. I turned to my dad and said, "I'm ready." I have no idea what he was doing but we both jumped back into the Jeep and headed up the mountainside.

There were so many beautiful scenic lookouts on the way up. I think we stopped at most of them. Each time I felt a little closer to

God, one step in front of the other, as if soaring like an eagle, allowing the winds to drive me to places I had yet to see. Not only in the physical, but I felt as though my soul was mounting up, assembling an irrefutable truth that was about to change my life. The mountains had the power to quiet my soul with constant serenity. It seemed as though the higher in elevation we got, the quieter the conversations in my head became and I realized the pauses of adoration grew to be longer as we traveled from point to point, providence to providence.

Our final destination for the day was with the tundra at the top of the Rocky Mountains. It was amazing. I couldn't wait to take off my shoes and walk across it with my bare feet. It looked like carpet. Something I loved to do was rub my feet on grass that felt like carpet. I remember spending hours with my shoes off trying to find the perfect patch of grass. There was nothing like it and my eyes were now looking at a landscape full of perfect patches of grass.

I couldn't wait to jump out of the jeep and make my way through

the carpet bed of tundra onto the rocks that overlooked the highest

peaks on our route. I took my shoes off and stepped off the trail

and onto the most comfortable grass I had ever felt. It was so

different. It was so thick my feet floated on top instead of sinking

deep inside. I felt as though I were walking on clouds and could

touch the sky. I made my way through the tundra and to the rocks I

wanted so desperately to climb.

I loved these rocks, they were discolored versions of gray covered

by spotted green mosses; they felt rough to touch and smooth in

some places, like the wind had worn them down over centuries.

Once I reached the top of the rocks, I found the perfect place to sit

and settle in for a while. I was so consumed by the beautiful

carpeted grass I had not realized what my eyes were about to see.

As I lifted my eyes up, I became a witness to the ageless wonder of

valleys and peaks, rising and falling, like an orchestra playing to an

audience of one, and for the first time in my life I saw how big

God really is and how very small I am.

I thought I must look like size of an ant to God and I couldn't

believe I still mattered to Him. He still thought of me even though,

in comparison, I was the size of an ant. I couldn't help but to

wonder how many thousands of ants I must have stepped on in my

lifetime; crushed beneath my feet and I never even thought of it. It

actually took my breath away to understand He, the God of the

Universe and the creator of all that was beautiful, thought of me. I

was nothing, to no one, from nowhere, yet He still thought of me. I

mattered. I had purpose. I was important and not because of me,

but because God thought of me. He could see me. He chose to talk

with me even though I never thought I deserved it. I had spent

most of my life believing I could never pray to God. I was a

terrible person; a beautiful, wonderful God would not want to hear

from the likes of someone like me. Yet, here I was nothing more

than the size of an ant to Him and here He was right smack in the

middle of me.

It wasn't until after I was full of "awe," overflowing with the

magnitude of His goodness, abiding in the presence of His majestic

wonder, that God made me keenly aware that the suffering I had experienced my whole life had a name. The name was depression.

In that moment the "whys" all disappeared. It no longer mattered

why I had depression or why I had suffered my whole life, but

what did matter is what God was speaking into my soul. He lifted

the veil and I understood that my depression had a disguise. I saw

myself like a sheep in wolves clothing. I had been trained to

protect the sheep that was hiding beneath; beneath the covering of

self-preservation. I had learned that no one would protect me so I

had to protect myself. I did that by whatever means was necessary.

At times this manifested into self-harm or attempted suicides,

because it was the one thing that I thought I had control over.

But not on this day, on this day the sheep had been sheared by

God. He had cut away the coat of anger, frustration, strife,

bitterness, and self-loathing, while the echoes of "poor pitiful me"

faded away. I understood my depression had been clothed in utter

selfishness because it had a ministry of one; it only cared about

itself. It never allowed me to think of anyone around me. I let my

past dictate every single decision I made and I was blind to it. I

was blind to my selfishness because it had been misconceived as selflessness for years. All of the sacrifices I made were never for anyone else. Every single sacrifice was made so that someone, somewhere, would love me. It was all driven by me. I knew I had been lied to. I had been deceived. I had been told that no one loved me. I was disposable. Not wanted. Therefore, I learned how to make everyone want me by becoming really good at camouflaging my selfish desires to be loved, with pretty colors of words that other people wanted to hear or masked by actions people wanted to see. I grasped the thickness of the veil I had lived beneath my entire life; my soul had been blinded by lies told by me and to me.

In that moment, it was as if the veil had been torn in two by truth. A Truth about a God who sees, who knows, and who loves anyway. A truth that told me He will never change His mind about me. He will always be with me; He will never forsake me. A truth that said I will never lie to you, no not ever, even if it hurts I will show you the truth, but I will also equip you to handle it. Let me lead because I am a God who can be trusted.

I felt as though I were face to face with God as He showed me He is the same God who gave me a Savior named Jesus. The Jesus in the Jesus Loves me song is the same Jesus who called me to follow Him. I closed my eyes and felt as though His arms wrapped around me. I knew His embrace was not like the briskness I felt in the air. It was warm and safe. Right there, on that rock, He broke me open and poured self-value and self-love inside me.

Have you ever received something that you never had before and didn't know you needed until after it was given to you? That was me. I did not even know I was missing it. I never knew what self-value and self-love felt like. I didn't even know it existed. I had never experienced it before but I knew this kind of love would never grow weary. This kind of love was full of power and strength. I could have fainted beneath the weight of what God was showing me, but I knew this kind of love was living on the inside of me. It was then I closed my eyes and felt as though I was soaring like an eagle. I saw the mountains on high and the permanence of creation as far as my eyes could see. His presence permeated every part of my being. The greatness of what I saw could not be measured by height or depth and for the first time in

my life I knew what it meant to cry happy tears. I was in awe of

God, His transcendence stirred my soul. Suddenly, I became

acutely aware of my own consciousness and the magnitude of

God's heavens. I felt as though He spread them open like a curtain,

and I rested there as if I were seated at the right hand of God, in

Christ, on the mountain top.

Chapter Six:
He Makes All Things Good

It was hard walking away from the tundra but I knew I would carry this moment in my heart forever. It had become a monument of permanence. It would always be a place of transcendence where I had encountered a true awakening; as if my soul had emerged from a deep sleep. The only way I can describe it is as a "shifting;" something prosperous had taken its rightful place inside of me. I could actually feel it. I walked away from there with peace inside my soul; something I had never felt before. A peace that superseded what I thought was true about my past, about my present, and about my future. It changed me. I had been given a new perspective. I knew this kind of transformation would carry me through a lifetime and, once again, I found myself in a place where I knew I would never be the same.

I stood up with my shoes dangling from my fingers tips. My toes pressed forward into the rock, my arms stretched out across the vastness of the sky. I climbed back down as I balanced gravity between the weight of my body and weight of my Spirit. This rock of transcendence had illuminated my soul. I felt as though I had become buoyant, floating downward like vapor. When I suddenly noticed there was a sign. I walked closer to the sign so I could read it clearly. It said, "Please do not walk on the tundra, it is like a tiny eco-system of a mini forest and takes ten years to repair itself when it is walked on."

Right then, right there, in the middle of my spiritual awakening I was taken down a few notches. My "rocky mountain high" was instantly put into perspective. I came down from the heavens to realize there is much work to be done and apparently that work must start with me. I thought to myself, "Let me do some earthly good before I destroy this tiny, mini eco-system that takes ten years to heal." I looked at my dad, as if I had just gotten into trouble, with my toes tucked deep down into the tundra, I jumped to the closest rock. I bounced between the rocks until my feet landed on the pathway that the national park had so graciously provided for its tourist.

I thought to myself, "How could I have missed the sign?" I mean, it was right in front of the rock that I just climbed. To my amazement, the answer came rather quickly and somehow I knew it was because, on my arrival, my soul was still blind. In the same way that I was physically blind to the sign, I was also blind to the truth. I was so focused on me and what I wanted that the sign had no impact on my physical sight. Therefore, it had no impact on my decision making ability. I couldn't see it because I was still blind.

It wasn't until I came down off of the rock that I had been given new eyes. My vision had been widened and my sight had been stretched further than my ability to see clearly, to see the truth, and recognize it for what it was. The question "why" had stretched my mind beyond myself as it explained years of turmoil, sadness, and suffering. In an instant, I realized depression had trained me. I had been manipulated by its control. It had robbed me of energy and enjoyment. It had taken my ability to be kind and filled me with frustration and strife. It had imprisoned me with suicidal thoughts of worthlessness and guilt. Guilt for all the things I wanted to do but never did and for all the times I wanted to say no but stayed silent instead.

Depression was my blindness. It made me see life through a mirror that only I could see. No one could come between my reflection and me. Only "I" mattered. Not on purpose, because it never revealed itself as selfish or self-seeking. How could it possibly show the trueness of its nature? The nature to fulfill a self-prophesying destructive pattern could never be revealed. It would be like a kingdom rising up against itself, which only brings defeat.

Depression was my kingdom. I had become the enemy and it was out to defeat me. It came to kill me. I stood there and thought of all the times I didn't succeed in my suicide attempts and I thanked Him. I thanked Him because I could see. I could see that life's circumstances had driven me into the sweet arms of a blinded lullaby, but now, now all of that had changed.

It had changed because the veil of blindness had been lifted by a heartfelt cry to know why I couldn't see the tiny little sign that said "Do Not Step" on the tundra. How could it be? How could it be that it was the first thing I noticed coming down from the rock? Like a magnet my eyes were drawn to it. I rushed towards it and couldn't wait to read it. It was as if I was seeing for the first time, full of exhilaration and thrill. I mean, who gets that excited over a sign in a national park? Well, I did and it was more than a sign to me. It meant that I finally cared about something outside of myself more than I cared about me. I cared about "tundra" but mostly I cared about this God that cared so much for me that He, the creator of the universe, would reveal Himself in the tiniest of details.

When we made it back to the jeep, my dad started a deep discussion about the amazing-ness of ecosystems and how they work. He went into great detail of why it takes ten years to repair. I listened to him talking about this biological community of interacting organisms and how their physical environments construct their own ecosystem. I sat listening and wondered how long it would take to repair me. How long would it take God to repair the damage that was done by years of "interacting organisms" that constructed my "physical environment"? What kind of ecosystem had been constructed in me? I wasn't sure what the answers were but I knew one thing. I knew the kingdom of depression had been destroyed by the truth and God was getting me ready for the "rebuild."

My dad is like a walking encyclopedia. I wonder sometimes if he has a photogenic brain, but it's one of the things I love about him. We are never short on conversation. He talked, I listened, and we drove further down the mountain pulling into the next camping site. We knew there was no way we were going to be able to drive off of this mountain in the dark. I pulled out the portable DVD player (because that's what we had back then) and put in the movie *Shrek*.

I loved that movie. I had never cracked up so much in my life, and as I watched, I remembered the couple that showed it to me.

Michael and Rachel, I loved these two together, they were like peas and carrots. There was only one difference, everybody liked them. I stayed with them at their home in North Carolina when I would visit TJ. Rachel and I were best friends and our sons would play for hours while we drank coffee and belly laughed. Michael was always an artistic marvel to me. He was intriguing but quiet. I always felt like he said a lot with only a few words and his actions always spoke louder. They both made me feel loved and accepted.

I meet them when they moved on the air force base during my first marriage. They were our neighbors and I instantly loved Rachel. There was no way anyone could meet her and not instantly love her. Her whimsical nature was full of love and laughter. She had an uncanny ability to love her life no matter what was going on in it and I admired her for that. When I met her, I had my own idea of who God was; it was simple and easy. My ideology was we are to love our neighbor as ourselves, and if we can do that we, will be all right. Rachel's idea of God was much better than mine. She explained God in simple enough terms for me to understand. She told me God was like a best friend; it was Him you wanted to have your first cup of coffee with when you wake up in the morning. I never forgot that. It stuck with me. It was like a seed that planted a desire, deep inside my heart, to have God as my best friend.

As we got ready to settle in, my mind kept thinking about what it means to be a best friend. I even answered myself; well, at least in my thoughts I did. I thought a best friend would be someone who is consistently there for me even if I am not always there for them. I thought maybe they would accept me and I mean all of me; both the good and the bad. Perhaps, a best friend would be honest with me even if it hurts. By this point, I was pretty sure my relationship with Rachel and Michael helped me define what good fiends really look like and what I can expect from them.

I realized it was getting cold outside and we wouldn't be able to keep the jeep running all night. We needed to save gas so we shut the jeep off, put the seats down in the back and jumped inside. We dumped both suitcases out, covered ourselves with clothes, and fell asleep watching *Shrek*.

The next morning the sun was rising but had not made it over the mountains yet. I threw a couple of sweatshirts on to layer up and opened the door to step outside. I started walking away from the jeep when I noticed there was a path, so I took it. It guided me to a small body of water. The water was so still, it was like a mirror reflecting the splendor of the mountains. It was so quiet, in the midst of this illustrious display of God's masterpiece.

I stood there in "awe," breathing in the coolness of the air and exhaling white vaporous clouds with each breath. At the same time, I remembered the joy I got from waiting at the bus stop when I was younger doing the very same thing I was doing right now. I smiled and think I even giggled a bit. I was in the moment and I was enjoying it.

It was something so small that I took great joy in as a child; I loved breathing the cold air deep into my lungs and exhaling the warmth from my body. I stopped doing it years ago; as a matter of fact, I hadn't even thought of it until that very moment. Why had I stopped enjoying something so small? I knew why I just hadn't said it out loud. I stopped because it reminded me of how my joy was stolen. How it was taken from me time and time again. The simple joy of taking in a breath of fresh air stolen by the chants of mean kids calling me "dirty pants" or some other derogatory name; all of whom were from a same small town where everyone knew who my mom was.

But not this time, I stood there unashamed and made an "O" shape with my mouth as I puffed the clouds out against the morning mist. The memory of them hadn't echoed in my soul. Looking back, I realize He had given me a gift. A gift to move past the past and be present in the moment and all I could say was, "Good Morning, God," with a smile on my face as far as the east is from the west. I stood there in "awe" of Him. There were no other words and, for the first time in a long time, there were no other thoughts. It was just me and Him enjoying the moment and the first light of day together.

The peace of His presence filled me up as I headed back to the jeep. I wondered what my dad was up to. I opened the car door and saw that he had his day old coffee in front of the heater vent trying to warm it up. Immediately, he began to tell me how amazing his morning was. He had seen a deer and it came right up to the jeep. He told me all about the doe and his visit with her. After waiting a few minutes, I asked my dad how long he'd been trying to warm up his coffee. He said, "About fifteen minutes." I knew right then it was time for us to find some fresh brew. We put the car in drive and continued on our way down the mountain. I would say about thirty minutes into the drive down we noticed on the right was an entrance to somewhere or something. The sign was obvious but at the same time we weren't quite sure if we were invited. It was made with huge wooden logs holding what appeared to be welded iron arching over the entrance which read "Grand Lake." The only signs I had ever seen like that were on movies and belonged to

ranches out in Texas somewhere. Nonetheless, we both looked at

each other and ventured beneath the arch into the unknown. The

trees felt like they towered over us as we drove further inside. It

did not take long to notice the huge cabin perched on the

mountainside as if welcoming our arrival.

We were both relieved and thankful. Relieved, because this place

definitely looked like public domain and coffee might soon be on

our horizon. Thankful, because we weren't actually trespassing and

were in the clear. That being said, we had no idea that God had an

amazing breakfast buffet tucked away at the bottom of the

mountains. There was yogurt, fruit, and granola, all of my favorite

things. Not to mention the endless cup of coffee. We had definitely

hit the jackpot. It was a goldmine and it was served up right buffet

style.

We filled our eyes with the grandeur outside of our breakfast window. It was amazing to see the beauty that surrounded us. It was Majestic in a way that cannot be explained. The mountains loomed over the lake below us. It was a reflection of what we had just experienced. It was as if we were perched on the side of the mountain eating breakfast maybe like a bird would in its nest. Although we were inside, I could still smell the freshness in the air; it was crisp and gave me chills from the top of my head to the tips of my toes.

We took our time and talked about how we wanted to come back to this place one day to stay for a while. It was rustically beautiful and natural among its elements. There was something special about it but both of us had the feeling that the road was calling our name, so we got our coffee cups to go and headed for the car. I knew we were going to visit my dad's family in Toole, Utah. That is where my Grandma Braun lives and the very town my dad grew up in with his brothers. The four musketeers, Uncle Bobby was the baby, and then there was Uncle Matthew, Uncle Mark, my daddyo, and

Uncle Marty who was the oldest. I couldn't wait to meet everyone.

It would be like it was the first time because it had been so long. I

didn't have much of a memory of any of them; except of course for

Aunt Carol who was Uncle Mark's wife.

They were just on the other side of the Rockies living in Sarasota

Springs, Utah which wasn't far from Toole, but they would be the

last stop. I couldn't wait to see Aunt Carol. I had not seen her since

I was very small. I am assuming I couldn't have been more than

three when I saw her last, but I never forgot the only memory I had

of her. I guess that's what happens when you are small. The bright

things in life illuminate your heart in a way that it can never be

forgotten. Don't get me wrong. I remember the "bad" people in my

life but I think that's what makes the sweet one's stand out all the

more. To me, Aunt Carol held a candle no one could blow out.

I sat in the car remembering her. I can still see it today, my sister,

Karen, and I standing in a bathroom mirror while Aunt Carol fixed our hair and makeup. She used a curling iron on my hair and I loved it. I can remember how beautiful I thought she looked but mostly I remember how kind she was to me. I told my dad about my memory and he laughed. He said, "Aunt Carol? Are you talking about the same Aunt Carol I know?" I said, "Yes!"

For the next several weeks, my dad and I hiked mountains, bathed in rivers, slept in tents, and stayed at Aunt Carol and Uncle Mark's house on the days we were back from the mountains. Uncle Mark took me down to the spa, which was a natural hot spring they had by the pool in their community. It was amazing. I could go there every night. Even when it was cold outside, "the spa" and heated pool made it all worth it. They even took us to the boat club where they had a huge RV and a boat. Uncle Mark taught me how to water ski. He never gave up on me even though I was ready to give up on myself. Every time I fell down, he would yell out, "Try again." Little did I know his words would echo in my heart for years to come!

It seemed like it took forever, but after a whole lot of tries, I finally got up on top of the water. It only lasted a couple of minutes but I felt victorious. It is amazing what a little tenacity will do. After skiing, I gathered my things and headed to the outdoor shower. I had never taken a shower outside. With the sky above me, the freshness of the air, and hot water pouring over my back, I felt so free. I loved it there.

My uncle and aunt did a lot for me. I don't know if they will ever understand the depth of my gratitude for the love and acceptance they showed me while I was with them. Not to mention, they both cracked me up the whole time. Laughter has a way of healing your heart when it's been broken for so long.

We went to Bryce, Zion, and Ophir Canyons, and any other canyons we could find; all while we were staying with Uncle Mark and Aunt Carol. As a matter of fact, it was them who talked us into going to Jackson Hole, Wyoming, and Yellowstone. I am so glad

they did. I got to see the vastness of the canyons, rivers, and

mountain ranges. I even got to experience the world's most famous

geyser, "Old Faithful," shooting up some twenty plus feet into the

air. To think, we were walking on top of the largest super-volcano

on the continent while we stayed in the valley of Jackson Hole,

Wyoming, nestled beneath the grandeur of the Teton Mountain

Range. All I could think of was, "Wow, pinch me," and, "Is this

real?"

Prior to this trip, there was nothing about me that wanted to get

dirty or be around any type of nature that could harm me. I guess I

lived under a blanket of fear even though I didn't realize it. God

did so much for me. I got to enjoy my life. I did what I could have

never imagined doing. It amazes me that I was never afraid. Not

once did I think about mountain lions, bears, snakes, spiders, or

any other creepy crawling things.

I think about all of those things now and, the truth is, it was a miracle that I never thought of those things then. It was a small miracle. So small that I didn't even know it was happening until I look back at it now. Today, I can say that "perfect love cast out all fear," but I didn't know that then. God loved on me and fear had no power over me. It felt as though God could see me and was smiling down on me and filled my soul with pure joy. I experienced so many different things for the first time and there were a lot of "first times" on this trip. I hadn't lived before now, and now that I know what it feels like to live, I never want to go back to who I was before I knew Him; before I knew the depth of His love for me.

When I think about all the moments when I could have been afraid, I am left in complete amazement. I mean, my dad and I had climbed up Ophir Canyon, which is near Tooele, Utah without any gear, just a backpack with granola and water in it. I had no idea what I was doing. I was in active training. Once, when we were coming down the side of the mountain it was incredibly steep and I had no idea how to lower myself without falling. I learned quickly

the higher you climb the more careful you have to be in order to

get down safely. My dad explained to me how to hold on to the

grass as I lowered myself down the mountain.

As I held onto the grass and trusted in its ability to hold me, I

thought about the years I lived in the valley and how noisy it was. I

thought about the constant chatter that consumed my mind and the

busyness I had been plugged in to. My mind was always going a

thousand miles a minute in every single direction at the same time

and nothing had the power to quiet it. No medication, no therapy,

and no relationship. I just learned the skills to manage living with

the noise.

But not this time, I thought about how I had never seen the heights

of life from the view of a mountain top until now. I felt as though I

had been immersed, as if swallowed whole, in the magic of

mindfulness. Nature had a way of quieting my soul and

transporting my thoughts into nothingness as my heart absorbed, like a sponge, the peace I found in solitude. The solitude in my mind, its chatter had been silenced and it finally quieted.

I slide down the mountainside, being mindful and present, until we made it to level ground. Together, we looked up behind us and my dad pointed to the spot we started to descend from. I couldn't believe my eyes when I saw it was about a twenty foot drop off of a cliff which explained why I told him, "There is nothing to hold on to." We looked at each other knowing it was a good thing we turned around and went back.

At the time, when we were up there on the mountain, in the thick of finding a safe way down, we had no idea of the dangers that lurked just beyond the edges. As I stood there looking at the cliff, I realized that it is God who protects me. He protects me from the dangers that lurk just beyond the edges of my life without me even knowing it. He allowed only what I could bare. He never let me break. He never let me fall to the point of no return. I was never

out of His reach. I remained wrapped in the palm of His hand.

Even though I experienced pain and suffering, through it all, it was

Him who kept me safe.

I stood there; my ears perked, I knew His voice. I recognized it

was Him speaking from within me and I felt His protection. I

understood it was not important, for me, to know everything. I

didn't need to know the details. I didn't need to know every single

lurking danger, and I didn't need to know every single memory of

a lost childhood. I could let it go and be grateful for memory loss.

He was protecting me from an ugly truth that could harm me. It

was what lurked beyond the edges and I did not need to fall off of

a cliff to find it. All I needed was Him, who reconciled my soul

with Himself, and He was more than enough.

Only seconds had passed when I heard my dad telling me that we

needed to follow the stream down the mountain because it would lead us back to the jeep. Little by little it became easier. Not only physically but mentally; I had finally conquered the noise. I was humbled by the silence. I had left the chatter behind as I learned a lot about conquering my journey as we overcame obstacles coming down off that mountain. I discovered stinging nettle which is a plant that causes a reaction in your body, making your skin feel like it is being stung with a thousand pin pricks at the same time. Apparently, it lasts for a few days. I learned to listen more than I speak and follow directions because my life would depend on it.

These lessons became repetitive as we hiked other mountains like I was in training for a "life" marathon and learning how to run my race. I thought about the resemblance between hiking these mountains and living life. The more we hiked, the more I understood that there would be obstacles and we would overcome those obstacles little by little. Mostly, I learned to listen, to follow, and to never give up. After all, we were in situations where we had no other choice but to just keep moving no matter how hard the trail got. The resemblance of these hikes and my life was uncanny.

We explored caves, and saw some of the most beautiful national parks in America. The interesting part is how much I learned about the character of God on this journey. Before we were ever born, God knew us. He knew me and my dad. He knew we would be right here, at this moment, at this time. God knew exactly what our hearts needed and it was Him who went about healing what was broken; not only in me but also in my dad.

I learned so much about God's character when I saw Him mending my dad's relationship with his family. I got to be a firsthand witness of my Heavenly Father's ability to transform our mess into a message.

The last time my dad was in Utah, about three years prior, he was an alcoholic and had been struggling with alcohol for about eight years. It was easy for me to understand that it takes a lifetime to build a strong bond with others but the power of addiction can destroy that bond in no time.

When we arrived in Utah, I learned that in the shadows of my dad's alcoholism was a wake of destruction, full of bad memories that littered the good ones. What I hadn't realized was everyone was expecting the worst of my dad, but, instead, they got his absolute best. He had recovered from his addiction by using the AA twelve-step program. My dad used to tell me how AA didn't allow him to actually verbalize who his God was. The program always required everyone to refer to Him as the "God of my understanding," but my dad would always say, "The God of my understanding and His initials are Jesus Christ." I love that about my dad.

His boldness was like no other; his words often like a Mike Tyson punch. They left you dazed and confused, not really knowing how to respond to your own hot air. Let's face it; not being able to name your "God" is nonsense. Nonetheless, I learned by watching

him to never let your past stop you from moving forward. He never

once let the stories that his family told about the years of his

alcoholism stop him or make him turn back to alcohol. He always

allowed them to voice their hurt without judgments but he also did

not allow those hurts to continue hurting himself.

Overtime, it was so obvious that each family member was amazed

at the changes in my dad. The hardness of their hearts from all the

years of disappointment had been softened. Perhaps, my dad's

living testimony planted seeds of hope in the soft terrain of their

hearts. I am still amazed that I got to be the one to witness my

Heavenly Father's handiwork. I watched as I saw Him restore

relationships for my dad and his family. I think it meant the world

to his family to know that my dad was good.

It was beautiful to be a witness but I am only privy to what I have

seen with my own eyes, and what I have seen is a God who makes all things good. The ugly stuff just seems to fade away into His glory. All while He uses it to make us shine even brighter. Now, I can see clearly. Now, I understand more than ever, that wherever we have come from, whatever we have done, or whoever did it to us, it pales in comparison to the light of His glory because that is where He makes "it" all good.

Chapter Seven:
Forty Days and Forty Nights

After four weeks of reconciliation, and time well spent with family, I was starting to get antsy. There was unrest inside of me, so I knew it was probably time to get back on the road. We headed back towards highway ten heading straight back to North Carolina. I knew enough time had passed but I also knew the journey wasn't over. After all, I still needed a final destination. Where would I go? Where is the place I would call home? Even though my head and my heart were full of questions, there was nothing that could stop us from taking our time and absorbing what was on the road ahead of us.

We left Bakersfield, California and headed towards Zion National Park. It would be our last stop in the great mountainous ranges of the west and I was excited to explore them one last time. We drove for a few hours before we arrived in Zion. The jeep started the climb up the side of the magnificent sandstone cliffs. The tires seemed to melt into the roads, as if they were one, winding snuggly against its monoliths gaps. The canyons were so wide the sunlight disappeared into its river carved gorges; to say that it was beautiful does it little justice.

There are not enough adjectives to capture the majesty of God's design. The paint brush of His spoken word casts all of this into existence. How could I measure the magnitude of this beauty in the simplicity of my words? I cannot. So instead, we stopped. There was no way we could continue driving. We pulled off at the closest sightseeing plateau. When we got out of the jeep my dad talked me into climbing over the edge of one of the barriers. He did a lot of that but it never really took too much convincing. I was ready for anything.

We sat there for a long time enjoying the final moments of absorbing the majesty of these Cathedral Mountains. After all, we were getting ready to say good-bye to them. We both sat there together, in silence, in quiet awe of creation. I am sure we were both pondering the magnificence of it all. I imagined God was smiling at us while we were taking in the air, feeling the grass between our hands, as we leaned against the cascading mountainside. It was different this time. There were no more what-if's churning in my mind, no more how-comes, just hushed whispers of a past that had lost its voice. I sat there overwhelmed by being fully present in the moment. I no longer had to conjure up the effort to be mindful, it just came naturally. I closed my eyes to breathe it all in and when I opened them back up, behold, a new site was in front of me.

I hadn't noticed it when we pulled up. I did not see it when we crossed over the barriers to find the perfect scenic spot. It wasn't until I opened my eyes that I realized I had been here before. I had seen this place. I asked myself, is this deja vu? Nope, not this time, I jumped up and told my dad to wait right there. I ran to the jeep, opened the door, and fumbled around beneath the front seat until my fingers found it. I gripped it tight and pulled it out. It was already folded open, so I couldn't see it. I couldn't see the cover. I closed it and there it was.

We were standing right smack dab in the middle of the cover photo on a road atlas I had bought two years earlier. I couldn't believe it. I ran to my dad to show him and sure enough we must have been in the exact same spot of the person who took that photo. It was incredible. I was left there with my mouth open in astonishment of a God who thinks of everything.

I stood there as if my spine were bolted to the earth, immovable for a moment, as I understood the completeness of a God who plans every detail to the fullest. I couldn't believe the map I was holding was the exact map God wanted me to buy for such a time as this. I didn't know I was going on a trip across country when I bought it. Standing there I knew it was Him who prompted me to buy it. At the time, I didn't even need an atlas. I just liked the picture on the cover and the memory of my dad teaching me how to read one.

It could only be God who knew exactly where the photographer stood to snap the picture that would be plastered on the cover of an Atlas that I was holding in my hands right now. It was God who provoked my dad to step over the security railing and encouraged me to come along. I stood there in the fullness of my Father. In the completeness of His plans, I just stood there in admiration of the magnitude of His inclusiveness.

I understood like I have never understood before that it is God, My Father in Heaven, who takes full advantage of every single thing in my life for one purpose; to love me so that I may indeed love others the way He has loved me. God has a plan and it is fully developed. I can consider it as good as done; as if it were finished from the foundations of the earth. I understood it is Him who chose me. It is Him who does all things to the glory of His goodness and for what? To share with me the plans He has for my welfare. Who am I? Who am I to be thought of by Him?

I had never felt so small in all of my life. The weight of what God was showing me gave me purpose and it was full of expression. The expression of His will for my life. He made me one with Him, one with Christ, as He watched over every little detail of my everyday life. He called me out from among the dead to do what? To share in His goodness, in His love, in His Mercy; God's own personal intervention made room in my rigid heart. I shared in the wholeness of His being and trusted in the outcome of His plans. The very same plans He had stored up just for me from the foundations of the earth.

Whatever leftovers of past remembrance that still lingered inside of me were gone. The awareness of the full and complete measure of who God is filled every empty space in my soul. I was full of the magnitude of what only God could orchestrate in my life. The presence of His power and grace, the fullness of believing in something I could not see was so overwhelming that the "awe" of

Him surpassed everything I ever knew of Him. In that moment, He became tangible, someone I could feel and touch and I knew I would never be alone again. He was going to see me through, and although I had no idea where I would end up, I was not afraid.

We came off the side of that mountain and headed into the Arizona deserts. It was dark by the time we arrived to some of the most beautiful night skies in the United States. The purity and depth of the ethereal blue reflected an altitude of the weirdest shades of purple. The deep violets of twilight reached from horizon to horizon. The stars beaming light streams were blanketing the sky. The beauty of it took my breath away.

As the sun rose, it felt as if we drove across the surface of the earth with waves of intense heat vaporizing the pavement ahead of us. I couldn't help but feel the heat of the Arizona desert as it held mysteries of grandeur with miles of hot dust-laden air ahead of us. The intensity of its sprays of whitecaps in colors of red, orange and yellow painted the desert skyline. As my eyes indulged in the secrets of this place, the screaming life of the Vegas strip interrupted my Indian summer visions and all I could think of was one word, NO.

Civilization at its finest never seemed more distorted than it did coming away from the clear night skies of the Arizona deserts. I did not want to hear the loudness of the Vegas strip. I wondered if anyone noticed what was happening in back alley ways, or street corners. Did they see the needle thrown in the street and people searching for them? Did anyone look up from their feverous assumptions of a time well spent? "Spent;" there's a word that explained everything in this place and there was nothing I wanted to see here.

I felt as though I had already seen it all. When I looked closely, I didn't see the pleasure; what I saw was the pain. As we drove through the streets, all I could feel was the darkness masquerading as light. The daylight hide the vibrancy of the Vegas lights bouncing off its streets and muted the attractions making them seem dull. For some reason, it reminded me of the stars in the desert and how the starlight made me feel pure, how it filled my heart with hope and expectation; while, the Vegas lights were man-made and had the potential to fill hearts with distraction, disappointment, and regret.

The truth was, I couldn't wait to get out of Vegas and it didn't take long to drive through it all. I couldn't help but think "to be such a small strip of lights and temporal glory it sure does have a huge impact on those who are stuck there." Nonetheless, our plan was to continue on to highway ten until we could cut off and hug the coast to drive through New Orleans, Louisiana, but Hurricane Katrina changed all that.

We heard the devastation on the news August 29, 2005. We had left North Carolina on August 4, 2005 and returned on September

5. At the time, we had no idea we would find our final destination on September 13, 2005. Nor did I know this journey would end up being exactly forty days and forty nights.

When we left, there was not a plan. There was no agenda and I had no idea there was a correlation in the scriptures. I do now and I think it is important to include that Jesus fasted forty days and forty nights, in the desert, after his baptism. (Matthew 4:2, Mark 1:13, Luke 4:2). The period of Jesus resurrection and ascension to heaven was forty days (Acts 1:3). Moses went up the mountain of God for forty days and forty nights (Exodus 24). So what does have to do with me?

I believe it was a period of testing, a time of reflection, and cleansing. I had to go through all of this to realize God had a promised land prepared just for me. He was equipping me with the tools I would need to step into the next part of my journey; self-worth and value. God was showing me who He was and what His character really looked like. I understood the truth and the truth is there is nothing I am going to do that will add to the cross and there is nothing I am going to do that will ever take away from it.

In other words, I could never add to Jesus and I could never take away from Him. He is complete and whole. He chose to become the way, the truth, and the life, and bring me into a perfect relationship with my Father in heaven. He has given me a way to find my life in Him. He is the source of all truth. He is the beginning and He is the end and He is all my in-between.

It was Jesus who fasted for forty days. It was Him who prayed, in the garden of Gethsemane, as great drops of blood dripped from His head from the anguish of knowing He would bear the burden of sin for all of eternity. It was Jesus who asked God to take the burden of bearing the cup away from Him; yet, laid His will aside to take up His Father's will instead. It was also Him who remained faithful and still remains faithful today. He was the one crucified for my sins so that I could experience what it feels like to be forgiven. He was the one who said, "It is finished," and gave up His Spirit as He died there on that cross. It was Jesus who our Father in heaven resurrected from the dead and ascended into Heaven. Why? Why did He do all of that?

I have the answer. I know it now, but I didn't know it then. He did all of that for the "hope that I might" come to know Him. To have a relationship with Him so that I "might" let His Spirit, the Holy Spirit, be my teacher. He had a hope; a hope that I might come to know Him as the giver and redeemer of my life.

Who has ever done anything for me with a "hope that I might" respond? No one! No one that is, except for Jesus. It took forty days and forty nights for me to bury the past and leave it buried. It took Jesus to show me He is the one who transforms my pain into cornerstones for His use in the future. He took what was meant to harm me and built a house inside my heart; filling every empty space with His love. The Father, The Son, and The Holy Spirit

dwelling in one place at one time with the hope that I might come

to join them.

Uncle Bobby, Baby
Jessica, Karen
(blondy), Me, Shelton,
Mikey (1yr)

Jessica, Mikey, Shelton
(no head), Karen, Me
(Silly Face), DaddyO

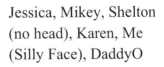

Mom at 21 and Mom at 49   Uncle Mark and Aunt Carol

Me at 6   Mikey   Jessica

Me at 4 with baby   Shelton
brother Mikey
                           Karen

                           Me at 8

Mermaid Stomping
Grounds

Chapter Eight:

New Beginning

The road was behind us, the mountains were a memory, and we would be crossing the North Carolina border very soon. I couldn't help but to reflect on what I had just experienced. It was fixed inside my heart as if something was raised inside of there. I couldn't describe the feeling other than to say I felt full. Like there were no more empty spaces, the vacancy signs had been removed, and I felt completely occupied.

The magnitude of my God and how much he cared about every single person in our journey echoed inside my heart. From those I shared Jesus with in the hotel lobbies and restaurants, to the relationships of my dad's family being restored. I knew my Father cared deeply about us all and I knew more than anything people mattered and so did their relationships. As I sat there in the passenger seat, not really knowing what the future held, I knew God never missed a day or a moment. He is with each of us always and what we think we lose in years, he gives us back in grace; a grace that has no measure and multiplies the moments that matter the most.

We arrived in North Carolina, pulling up into my ex-husbands driveway. My number one priority was to see my son, TJ. I missed having him with me during the weeks away but I also knew what God had done inside of my heart and how much I had changed. I wondered if anyone would notice what happened to me on the inside by looking at me from the outside. They didn't, but, honestly, I did not think they could. This was all new to me. I was about to come face to face with myself and all the decisions I ever made. I had no idea how God would take what I had broken and turn it into a multitude of new beginnings.

My ex-husband, Eric, and his wife, Shelia, had always been good to me. I appreciated who she was in my life and in our son's life. I don't think she could ever relate to a mother who would walk away from their child because of the mother that she was. She is amazing. I used to refer to her as the "soccer mom." Shelia tried to

encourage me with her words. Once, she asked me if I was afraid.

At the time, I didn't really know the answer to her question, but

now I do. I was afraid that I could never be the mom I wanted for

my son. She was everything I wanted him to have and I was

thankful for that.

I listened to Shelia's supportive words but never felt like I could

compare to the amazing mom that she was. I always wanted what

was best for my TJ even if that meant being without me. I mean, I

had the capacity to be the fun mom. I could be the weekend,

holiday, and summer mom, but it was difficult being the everyday

mom. When TJ was in kindergarten, I failed miserably at making

sure he had breakfast before school. It was the one goal I wanted to

achieve and I couldn't seem to manage even that small of a task

much less be responsible for his daily needs. I was afraid. I was

afraid to fail as a mom. I wanted him to have the perfect mom and

there was nothing about me that was perfect. I had yet to realize it was caused by the lack of mothering in my childhood and a deep

desire to protect him from my brokenness.

I was happy Eric and Shelia were always so easy in dealing with

me. They often let TJ leave with me whenever I would show up to

get him. So, we drove back to my brother's house. It was only

about an hour's drive. We pulled into my brother's driveway. A lot

had changed. I was returning a new person and was excited to

share all that I had seen. My brother Mikey and his wife, Kim,

were happy to see us all and welcomed us with opened arms. He

put up with a lot while I was gone and he did it all to protect me;

just like a brother would.

Mikey and Kim had become like surrogate parents to TJ. They

really do love him like their own and I love them for that. I can see

now, how God was providing for my son what I lacked to give

him. It was God who was the one taking good care of my TJ and

loving him in all the ways he needed; through other people in his life. We stayed in North Carolina long enough to spend the weekend with TJ. I briefly looked for jobs. I prepared my resume but it didn't feel as though we were ready to settle in. The trip felt unfinished for some reason and I hadn't yet come into understanding why.

It wasn't until my older sister, Karen, had called from Florida to ask why we hadn't made it to her house yet. I told her I didn't think we would make it. At which point she said, "You mean you drove all across America and back and you are not coming to Florida to see me." I hadn't even thought of it from her perspective before, but now that she said that, I felt like I needed to go and see her. I mean, when we left New Jersey I remember feeling like I was packing for Florida. My dad and I even talked about going to Florida but I was still unsure.

The truth is, I wanted to stay in North Carolina, but I had an uneasy feeling about it for some reason. I remember telling TJ I was going to Florida but that I would be back, which turned out not to be true. There are moments in life when you wish you could take back your words but you can't. At the time, I had no idea I would make the decision to stay in Florida and this decision would reinforce the negative feelings of "not being heard" in TJ's heart.

I didn't know the impact my words would have on his heart when I told him I felt like God wanted me to stay in Florida. I didn't have the understanding or ability to explain clearly what I meant when I said those words. Therefore, I believe those same words told him that I chose God over him. I am not sure but what I do know is my choices affected my son's ability to feel heard or, as it was, unheard; as if to say TJ's voice didn't matter, it was another sign that strengthened a negative message and I had no idea of the collateral damage I was leaving in the heart of my son.

I didn't realize that a twelve-year-old couldn't possibly understand the depth of what I meant. I had no idea there was a good chance that the enemy would use the ignorance of my words and the maturity level of his age to reinforce the idea that "God" was a "God" who takes away, which was not the message I wanted him to hear. At the time, I don't believe that either one of us realized the years it would take to work through the pain of feeling rejected. I am not even sure if we knew how to name the feelings that surfaced from being rejected, but I believe it was an unintentional consequence of ignorance.

Clearly, it was never my intention to be the source of making him feel rejected, but I was and I knew it. However, that didn't stop God from comforting my heart as I dealt with the pain of feeling guilty for my mistakes, especially those that affected someone I love.

How did God bring me comfort? He did it through understanding. Somehow, I just knew, deep down inside my heart, that most people in their twenties do the exact same thing I did and were experiencing much of the same things TJ was. Perhaps I may never

know exactly what he went through, but I know what my heart was

telling me and I know it was not easy for him. Nonetheless, God is

still God and He would use the very thing that was meant to harm

TJ for his good.

The truth is, we are going to make mistakes, but we shouldn't give

our mistakes more power than our ability to change, to grow, or

become better. Yes, it is also true our mistakes have the ability to

make us stagnant, if we let them, we will become like stale old

water, putrid from the smell of becoming dormant with guilt. Did

you hear me, "If we let them"?

I think it is important to share with you the understanding I gained

about the decisions I had made in the earliest parts of my journey

with God. I want you to know I lacked knowledge and that lack

had unintentional consequences. It took time; lots of time to

understand who I was in Christ and to learn the new identity I had living on the inside of me. Without a doubt I am sure I am not

finished but that is what I am here for and that is what you are here

for too.

I had to learn the words that I had used, the actions I had taken

before I ever knew Jesus, had built a temple in my heart, but not

the kind that Christ builds. It was a temple built to keep people out.

I had spent years constructing exterior walls as a means of

protection. Those walls stopped whatever had the power to intrude

on my feelings. I thought I was always in control of what I allowed

through the doors of my heart. Often times, in order to stop the

intruding forces of unwanted emotions, I dabbled a bit in

therapeutic delusional-ism, finding ways to manipulate my own

mind into believing a life built on fallacy.

I claimed liberty; that I was free but I recognized the chains from a

past that I longed to forget. I understood what had happened. I had

walked many miles in these same shoes and wanted so desperately to keep myself from traveling the same old roads. I was bound to a temple that was supposed to keep me safe and secure but instead it had become a prison in my mind, convincing me, all the while, that I was free.

I could see the parallel. My son's decision making looked a lot like my own. The very things I wanted to protect him from were the very things that crouched at his door. Although our childhoods were not similar, somehow, the enemy managed to send him the very same messages he had sent to me for twenty-nine years. The goal of the enemy was to accomplish three things both in my life, in my son's life, and anyone else's life for that matter which is to steal, kill, and destroy.

I wonder if all the "temples" that we build to protect ourselves are similar in design. Do we worship at the throne of idols without even realizing it? Does your temple look like mine and if it does, does that even matter? I may not know the answer to those questions but I can tell you the construction of the temple inside my heart was hard, harsh, and always turned inward. It had been designed to imprison. It's architecture founded on shame and confusion. Its very nature was a command of disgrace inflicted on me by the pain of never feeling good enough. The charge of my crime always before me like gullied ravines carved out by the torrential rains of abuse. The wounds of my prosecution were inscribed on the temple walls of my heart; by the hands of those who hurt me. It was a pain that sought only to destroy me and forced me to long for what has already been stolen.

I refer to it as a temple because that is where I worshipped. As crazy as that sounds, it is true. Not because I wanted to worship the framework of every bad thing that had ever happened to me and every bad thing that I had ever done. I worshipped it because I had spent years making it greater than God. I had spent all of my time making my issues bigger than the One who knitted me in my mother's womb. I think what bothered me the most was that I felt as though I could see it all happening to the one I tried so desperately to protect, my son. The pain of watching his struggles and allowing him to go through them, the way he needed to, all while trusting God to work it all out for good was definitely a process. The truth is I wanted God to supernaturally pass the process and do it in my timing. I was looking for a microwave answer to a slow cooker problem.

After everything we had been through, how could I share with him the hope that I had found? It wouldn't come with words because over the years "my word" had been raked over the coals, burnt up with the ash. It could only come in the form of time. I had no idea that it would be two years before his heart was soft enough to agree to come see me in Florida and this process could finally begin. Fortunately, by then, I had been fortified by truth. The truth I had found in His word and I studied it daily because I needed it.

I needed it because the temple I had built in my heart had taken twenty-nine years to build and God knew the truth was the only thing that could help me. The truth is the foundation of real freedom. Free from the lies that I would tell others but mostly the lies that I would tell myself. The truth has the one promise that could never let me down. It always had to deliver because it brought what was hiding in the darkness into the light. The truth is the very nature of my Heavenly Father who cares so deeply for me that He would be mindful of my needs, of my frailty, and handle me with such care. He never revealed to me more than I could handle; it was always just enough that my faith would get me through. This Father of mine, so delicate with the revelations He shared with me, was the same One who marked the dimensions of the universe with the words "let there be light," the one who laid the earth's foundation, who halted the seas that bowed to the shoreline, it was Him who burst light forth from the morning star, and provided a way where there was no way. It was Him who brought the rivers that filled the dry places in my heart.

It is Him who gave His son as the ultimate sacrifice for all sin, as far as the east is from the west and the past is from the future, sin has been removed forever. Its power stripped from the foundations of the earth, exposing the truth of the One who came to save me. He was the only One who loved me enough to die for the hope that I might come to know Him. There is no other love like this love. There is only One Love that had the ability to open the door to the throne room in heaven. There is only ONE LOVE who brought the throne room down from its celestial home and placed it inside my heart, but how did it get there?

Let me tell you how. Let us journey back when the temple in Jerusalem was bustling with the preparations for Passover. You are probably thinking what in the world does this have to do with this girl's story, but I invite you to stick around. I promise it will be worth it.

People had filled the temple courts with cattle, sheep, and of course, doves for those who couldn't afford the elite sacrificial elements. As Jesus entered His Father's house, His heart was filled with great energy in pursuit of His cause. The zeal to make things

right forged into one purpose, the creation of a whip made with

cords. He flipped tables, and scattered the coins of money changers

as he exposed the people who bought, sold, and exchanged money.

He demanded the den of thieves and vipers stop turning his

Father's house into a market.

The only thing the people could do was respond with, "what sign

can you show us to prove your authority to do such atrocious

acts?" His only response was, "I will destroy this temple, and I will

raise it again in three days." They replied, "You think you will

destroy and rebuild this temple that has taken us forty-six years to

build?"

In that moment, the disciples did not understand what Jesus was

talking about. Like so many other times Jesus' words would not

make sense until Jesus died and was resurrected. It wasn't until

then the disciples remembered what Jesus said on the day he drove out the money changers from the temple. It was in this moment

they realized that Jesus is the Temple. It was Jesus who faced the

harsh reality of God's people who had exchanged his Father's

house for a god of lessor value. The truth is, He destroyed the

temple and He destroyed all that the temple stood for. He

destroyed the foundations from which it was erected. The temple,

which was once the center of worship and sacrifice, could no

longer stand in the face of the cross. Its laws and obligations

accommodating sacrificial requirements were utterly abolished

with one action. It was the edifice of the King's crucifixion. This

action exalted the one name above all names, Jesus who was nailed

to the cross, who lived, who died, and who rose again.

In this moment, the same moment that I am reading this story from

John Chapter 2:13-22, I am confronted with every moment that I

have exchanged who my Heavenly Father is with what I have done

or with what has been done to me. In other words, I am forever one

decision away from choosing the cross, which covers me, or

choosing temporary satisfaction which is fleeting; never sustaining the kind of redemption that only comes from knowing what Christ has finished. He is the open door to the Father who loves me.

I sat there staring at the scriptures as I learned of my Jesus. I am brought to my knees in awe of the One who thought so highly of me. It was Him who took down the temple I had built inside my heart. He saved me from the fabrication of lies that were built by an enemy who hated me without cause. He abolished the laws of what this life had taught me. His truth revealed the unspoken obligations of perfection and ripped them from the framework of my soul. It was Jesus who removed the foundations from which I was born and gave me a new life; a life worth living in the shadows of His glory.

He destroyed the temple that was inside my heart, in order to rebuild it. If I were calculating it like a human would, I might say it took forty days to destroy the temple that I had spent twenty-nine years building. The truth is, the moment Jesus said, "It is finished," as He hung there on the cross, the earthly temple was destroyed.

I knew I would be faced with the destruction I had left in the hearts of those I loved, but I also knew He was with me. The old temple had been destroyed and a new one built in its place; a place where God transforms the ordinary into the extraordinary. A temple built, with love, full of corridors that I had not yet discovered, doors that had not yet been opened, and store houses full of gifts that I had not yet asked for.

I knew Jesus was the temple that was raised inside my heart. I knew He was the reason I was full and this relationship with Him was worth exploring. I also knew, even though I didn't, it would be Him that would restore, redeem, and replenish, more than I could imagine. He would restore the relationships that I had lost. He would multiply the time that had been wasted. In knowing Him, I knew I would find a lifetime full of mercies; like the sunrises every morning, I had a chance to live daily and bask in the grace of new

beginnings.

Chapter Nine:
The Baptism

I left North Carolina with an understanding that the temple in me had been raised with a purpose, but I did not understand the fullness of what I had experienced, of what He had shown me. I knew He was living inside of me. He had filled me with His Spirit. I had been baptized by His love and I knew I had every right to the Kingdom that He paid for. The entrance into the throne room was mine. At the time, I had not yet read the scriptures in John Chapter 3 verse 5. Therefore I did not know that Jesus said, "What is born of the Spirit gives birth to the Spirit." I did not know that Jesus promised to build His church on the rock of who He was, like it says in Matthew Chapter 16 verses 16-18. The scriptures reveal that Peter was not his original name. Jesus gave him that name because He knew His Father would reveal to Him who He was, The Messiah, The Son of the Living God, and that was the rock that would build the church, but I also did not understand that "I" was the church.

I was full and I felt like I lacked nothing but what I lacked was

knowledge. Over time, I have learned that knowledge comes when

I seek His truth above all else. It is when His word has the final say

in how I feel, in how I respond, and how I deal with those around

me. This only happens over time, and, with experience. Above all

else, I know God's grace is sufficient to keep me while I am

learning. After all, I could never be held accountable for what I do

not know and living life with people, in relationships, is the only

way to learn how to be accountable to God for what He chooses to

teach us through them.

The truth is, I had not yet learned how to love others the way

Christ loves me. I could only learn to do that with, time (t--------i---

-----m--------e), seed (planting what I learn in His word in the fields

of my life), and harvest (reaping what I have sown). Just like the

farmers in a field, preparing the land for a crop, I had just begun

plowing. In the beginning I made a lot of mistakes, but I was full of zeal for His love for me and I wanted the world around me to know it. I wanted them to experience the same love that Jesus had given me because I knew that what He had given me He had also given them. The only difference was they didn't know it yet.

My dad and I arrived at my sister's house at night. It was pitch black outside in the middle of Florida's Estero Aquatic land preserve which is where my sister lived. They had bought ten acres of land and built their dream home with a winding driveway, a heart shaped pond, and an in-ground pool. She had come a long way from the broken down shacks and trailers parks we left behind in North Carolina.

Other than the very brief encounter with each other at our mom's funeral, we hadn't spent time together since 1995, when I drove through Ohio and stopped by an apartment she had after she got married to her husband, Jay. They are funny together and made me feel welcomed. She had made a lot of plans for us to get to know

Southwest Florida. I remembered the first sunset she took us to on Bonita Beach. The brilliance of the white sand laden with shades of pastels from all the broken seashells blanketed the shoreline. They cascaded into the blue as the sun's reflection off of the Gulf reminded me of a million little diamonds floating on top of still waters.

The sun was starting to set and the skies filled with a million shades of pink. It reminded me of all the pink sunsets I had seen across the country, mostly from the window of my jeep. The deep colors of fuchsia radiated upwards from the surface of the ocean, fading into shades of orange and yellows. The sky's pallet was full of the purest shades of aqua. Nothing was left untouched. The mountainous clouds floating above us, growing ever higher as the sun settled into the velvet like teal lining on the horizon. The water was calm, much like my soul. It was quiet as I stood there looking out over the water.

I thought about how we had only been here for a week but I knew I had somehow found my way to the place I would call home. It would be the very first place that I would plant roots and grow. Even if I didn't really understand the depth of what I was feeling at that time, I knew I had arrived and it made me wonder what "home" would really be like.

We headed back to my sister's house as I told her what I was feeling. She responded with, "I am not ready for you to settle in, I have too much planned to show you," but I was anxious to find a job and begin again. I couldn't be a floater forever and we had already been on the road for more than a month.

I don't think she was happy that I wanted a job so quickly. Nonetheless, the following morning she handed me the help wanted ads from the local newspaper and believe it or not, I sent out my resume and had an interview in less than a week. Truth be told, I had one interview and started working in less than fourteen days after our arrival. The days leading up to my job allowed my sister and I to catch up on old times, but it is strange how spending so much time with her brought up a lot of old memories.

What we both learned was that while I thought she had it better than me, she thought I had it better than her; we both had it bad. We learned it was pointless to try to out win each other with our war stories. We were hurt and we were doing the best we could with our pain. She shared with me how she went through the teen challenge program and how it really opened a door for her to have a personal relationship with our Heavenly Father. I got to share with her what I had just experienced going across country and she understood where I was in my journey. One night, I don't even know if she remembers, but she told me, "right now you are full of zeal. You are in the stages of having and knowing "your first love" but that would soon wear off and you will get back to the real world."

I never said anything to her, but later that night I cried. She broke my heart with the most devastating news I could ever receive. I wept at the idea that I would somehow, one day, walk away from this amazing love that was so precious to me. It hurt so badly and I begged God to never let me go. I told Him I wanted Him to always be my first love and to protect me from ever losing the kind of love I had in my heart for Him. I was afraid that I would mess this relationship up just like I had done so many others, but I felt as though He held me there as I poured my hopes, dreams, and fears out into His arms.

What my sister and I discussed during those weeks was important. We had to face what had been hiding in our hearts all these years, but we also shared in God's word. We got to study together and talk about what the word meant and what applying God's word to our life looked like. It was an important time and the starting point of our Father repairing what had been broken all those years ago.

She supported me no matter what; just like she had always done.

She helped us find an apartment in a neighborhood about forty

minutes from her house, which was pretty close considering where

she lived. It was on a golf course and it was the first place I got to

call home. I used to refer to my bedroom as my prayer closet. It

was a place of sanctuary; it was where I retreated to read, to study,

and to worship Him and when I was home, that was my favorite

pastime.

After work, my dad and I would watch the sunsets from Bonita

Beach about three times a week. It was beautiful every single time

we went. The sky filled with hews of pink from fluorescents to

subtle nudes and it felt like they called my name every afternoon

around three. It didn't matter what I was doing, my mind would

wander to the sandy oasis of God's good nature. How could I not

think about how remarkable they were? There was never one like

the next, uniquely created every evening for the majesty of the

Heavens; just like we are uniquely made for God's goodness, so

were the sunsets. I believe watching those sunsets guarded my heart against being sucked back into mundane mindsets while they kept my hope alive with the majesty of God's goodness.

The days seemed to last forever in Florida and I couldn't wait to escape the confines of corporate America and head for the beach. When we got there I never bothered to change my clothes. I would just walk out into the water, fully clothed, lay back on the sea's surface and float. I would stare up at the clouds above me and let the water fill my ears, drowning out the noise around me. My life had never been quieter and I had never been more at peace.

As we enjoyed everyday living to the best of our abilities, life seemed to carry on, as life does, from one day to the next. The "drudgery" of work was motivating, but I was more excited about finding a home church. I had never had one before and couldn't wait to find one. So, we went about looking and were invited to my niece's church. It was a very small community church. It probably had about fifty people in attendance. I don't really know what I was expecting. Maybe I wanted the feeling of being there to resemble some feeling I had gotten on top of those mountains, but it didn't. The people were nice, and although we would ultimately choose to go somewhere else, this was the place I met my first friend in Estero, Florida. She was crying outside of the church after service and I wanted to help. So, I asked her if I could pray for her and that is what we did. We prayed together, exchanged phone numbers, and have continued our friendship throughout the years.

We probably went a few more times to that tiny little church before my dad heard a story about a pastor in a Baptist church close to where we lived. He heard the pastor had a big heart and opened the church's doors to shelter an alcoholic, not for just one night but for six months. The pastor opened the doors to the church, gave him a place to sleep, food, and gave up his own personal time to help the man get sober. This pastor chose love and he didn't choose to love the easiest person of character. He chose to love someone who was in need and someone who was struggling at the bottom of their barrel. It was the "Jesus" living inside the pastor who reached in to help pull a struggling alcoholic out of the pit of their destruction that my dad and I fell in love with. He was the heart of First Baptist Church of Estero and that was the first church we found and would call home in southwest Florida.

I knew it was the one the moment we walked beneath that old southern style steeple and through those sanctuary doors because it felt like home. I knew the leader of the church loved broken people, Jesus loved broken people too, and that I would "fit in" just fine. The truth was I was excited to go "home," to feel like I was in my "Father's house." I can tell you this, one of the first things I did was take my shoes off under the pew and rub my feet on the carpet of the sanctuary's floor. It made me feel closer to Jesus; like I had just kicked off my shoes after a long day of work.

I was so absorbed with God that it was easy to forget about the people around me. I mean, it wasn't that I ignored them. I was always happy, smiling at everyone, taking sermon notes in my journal, kicking my legs up in the pew like I was sprawled out on my living room sofa, and couldn't wait to get to church on Wednesdays and Sundays. The truth is, I didn't know any better; no one had taught me "Sunday etiquette." I just knew one thing, I couldn't wait to get to my Father's house as soon as the doors opened. It was my home and the people made me feel welcomed there. Most of them were much older than I was and dressed much nicer than I did, but they never made me feel bad about myself. They accepted me the way I was and that made all the difference. This was my foundational church. It is where I congregated with others who loved Him like I did. I was encouraged, edified, and built up in my faith. It is the place I learned to seek and I sought answers from those who knew more than I did. Those who had lived longer than I had and had seen their prayers answered. I was gleaning from the beauty of solid relationships in Christ, learning to live inside the walls of a church, but longing for what was outside of it. I wanted to tell the world of my Jesus but had no idea how to bring it out of the church and plant it inside the hearts of broken people. So I continued to listen, to learn, and to grow, little by little, step by step, through relationships inside of Estero Baptist Church.

I can remember this one time that I was sharing something I had found in the word and the person interrupted me with these words, "wow look at your countenance." I did not even know what that meant, so I asked him, "What do you mean?" He said, "You are glowing," and I said, "How could I not, with a Savior like Jesus?" I think I baffled people and probably scared more than I helped in the beginning. I mean, I was so passionate about my Jesus that even my pastor called me a Jesus freak, in a jokingly kind sort of way.

I spent most of my free time asking God to lead me. I had such a childlike faith. When I think about it today all I can say is, "Thank You Father for protecting me in my innocence, especially, in the early days." My favorite thing to do was to wake up and ask Him what He wanted me to do that day, and if I didn't hear anything I would get in my car and drive around asking for Him to direct me.

Do I turn left or right? I just went driving without a specific

destination and turning whichever way I felt like He was leading. I

think about how silly that is now, but in the beginning He met me

right where I was.

Now, I am not suggesting for anyone to do what I did; I am just

sharing with you my story. I even remember once I showed up at

somebody's house in the middle of nowhere. When I got out of my

jeep the dogs, with an "s," started barking. I cannot believe, in

spite of my fear, I unlocked the gate, stepped inside the yard,

closed the gate behind me, and walked up to the door. I had made

it that far and nothing attacked me. I thought to myself, "Okay I'm

good," so I knocked. As she struggled to hold back the beast from

tearing the door down, she managed to step outside. I noticed her

frailty and her age. She appeared to be lonely and I thought to

myself, "She's the one." My first words were, "I believe I am here

because God lead me to your door. Is there something you might

need?" I got to spend the next few hours listening to her story,

praying with her, and sharing with her the gospel that Christ had so
freely shared with me.

Even though I found her hap hazardously, God is still good. He
saw her and He knew my heart. It was Him who was faithful to
both of us. I have to tell you, I don't think I have ever shared that
story with anyone, and not because the bible tells me to not let my
left hand know what my right hand is doing, but because it was a
measure of the uniqueness of His grace.

It was a moment I got to see God move in the miraculous. Not only
did His sovereign grace keep me safe but He answered my heart
cry to share Jesus. I mean, I don't think I had to almost get lost and
go searching in the bowels of southwest Florida to find someone to
share Jesus with, but God met where I was and perhaps it was a
living parable for me. The truth is, I found her in the depth of
wilderness much like where Jesus found me. I was so lost inside
myself, by myself, in my own mental wilderness that perhaps, just

maybe, the desire to find someone who was lost played out in a real physical sense in my life. I mean, I went looking for someone among the marshy swamps in the sub-tropics of Florida. It was a physical wilderness but I found someone out there who was very much in the middle of her own spiritual wilderness. I may never know how that moment impacted her life but I will always remember how it impacted mine.

I learned to look outside of myself, to be led by faith, knowing God was trustworthy, and to touch the heart of someone else through the power of presence. I just showed up. I was the one person in the world who was present, who knocked on her door, and sat with her on her front porch. This incident planted a seed in my heart to never forget the power of being present in someone else's life. I will never forget how God shows up, how He sees, knows, and loves us all. My soul prospered on that day and a new heart cry was created inside of me, "Oh Lord, please let me keep showing up, wherever You need me that is where I want to be." I felt the heart of my Father and in feeling that, I felt blessed beyond measure. I was given an opportunity to sit with a stranger, even if it was for just a little while. I may never know if it changed her life but I know it changed mine.

I knew I could never find that place again; I didn't even try, because I knew it was a miracle that I managed to find my way home. The truth is, looking back, I probably would not recommend that for anyone. I think God kept me safe in my child-like faith. I mean, I prayed my way through that trip and I knew my heart was right. I wanted to find someone that was lost so they could find their way to Jesus and I believe that is exactly what happened.

The truth is, I was on a journey and I was looking for my "niche." I wanted to find the one person that needed to hear my story, but that wasn't the only thing I tried. I was determined to love others and so I would think of different things I could do that would share "love" with a hurting and dying world. This idea sent me to the local children's hospital. I would walk around with a canvas bag full of crayons and as the sick children passed through the halls I would let them color and sign my bag. Their smiles said it all. I think they loved it because it was something out of the ordinary. No matter what I did, it felt like God was always opening doors; especially, when I loved others, for the sake of "loving others."

Over the years, I have learned anytime we are going about doing what is good, it pleases our Father in Heaven because He is good. Good is who He is; His very own nature at work through us. The truth is, goodness is a fruit of the Holy Spirit living inside of me. It is the living proof of captivating the magic found in the supernatural goodness of our Savior Jesus, who spent His life going about doing good everywhere. He gave sight to the blind, healed the sick, and set free the captives. He proclaimed the year of the Lord's favor and I am here to tell you this is your year, your moment. Remember, He is the epitome of all that is good and the very beginning of the truth of the Good that lives in each of us. If we can learn to follow Him, to follow the promptings of goodness, we will find Him in the whispers of our lives and be a witness of the His amazing glory.

If I am honest, what I really wanted was to work for my Father in Heaven and not have to go to a mundane job; although, I was grateful I had one. I mean, that job provided for me and it wasn't a bad job. I just never felt like I fit in there and I did not have the freedom to share Jesus the way I wanted to, but I always managed to squeeze Him in there some way, somehow. It is so interesting how most people want to hear about Him but the "rule-makers" do not like it. I remember the first time I ever fasted was at my job. When I felt physically weak, I would go to the bathroom, sit on the floor and pray my way through it. Every time, I was strengthened to continue for another day. Once, when I was taking out the garbage, I was looking up at the trees above me and swore they were in total worship to my Heavenly Father. It was like the sounds they made, the bustling of their leaves was like music to His ears, and it was as if they knew Him in the same way I did.

The months went by so quickly; we had spent our first holidays in Florida which really felt weird to me. It wasn't even cold and I really wanted to wear a sweatshirt. I was so excited that Aunt Carol and Uncle Mark were coming to visit us, and my dad made arrangements for me to be baptized in water while they were here. I met with the pastor and he told me what I had to wear. I asked him if he minded if I wore my t-shirt and ripped up jeans because I wanted to be baptized the same way Jesus found me. He really didn't care. They just had me put a white robe on over my clothes.

It was Sunday, January 8, 2006. To be exact, that was fourteen years, four months, fifteen days, twenty-two hours, and thirty minutes ago. It was the most amazing experience I have ever had. It was also the same day as a 6.9 magnitude earthquake just off the coast of Greece in the Eastern Mediterranean Sea. I want to say the Heavens and the earth shook much like my entire body did standing in the baptism pool of my church. I am thankful no one died in that earthquake, but I am pretty sure when my pastor submerged me beneath those waters, the old had surely passed away, and the new had come.

When I came out of the baptism pool, I knelt down on the floor as soon as I got to the bottom of those steps and I wept. I sat there in silence with my face to the wall and my body crouched to the floor. Trembling from head to toe and not because I was cold but because I was overwhelmed by His presence. It was as if He was there with me, and I was bowed at His feet in awe of Him who loved me, but He wasn't standing there next to me. His arms were not wrapped around my shoulders. I didn't see Him on the outside but I knew He was standing on the inside of my heart, and I squeezed myself as I held onto who I knew He was. I was reminded of the love He gave to me and the value of my worth. I thanked Jesus for everything. I thanked Him for making me new on the inside and for showing me that He could be trusted to renew the outside.

I got to my feet knowing I had been, officially, baptized in the name of the Father, Son, and the Holy Spirit. I had confessed to the world as a witness that I was, indeed, dead to my old nature, buried in Christ, and resurrected from the grace into a new life, born of the living water I had found in Christ.

Chapter Ten:

Love Lesson

After the baptism, I was asked by the pastor to share my testimony at the six o'clock meeting that same Sunday evening. I would tell them all of the most amazing Love I had ever experienced. I would share how I had never felt love the way Jesus had loved me. He was my knight in shining armor, my prince, who came to my rescue and swept me off my feet. I was determined to make Jesus my main squeeze for the rest of my life and I would proclaim my undying love for him from the pulpit.

When we went home, I spent most of the afternoon preparing what I would say. I wrote it out word for word and planned on reading what I had written to the church, but God had other plans. The hours went by quickly and before I knew it, it was time to go. I actually left the notebook at home and hadn't realized what I had done until the pastor called me to the front to share.

The anticipation was building inside of me as I got to my feet. It wasn't that I was afraid, the butterflies in my stomach felt more like frantic excitement. My eyes were laser focused on the pulpit in front of me. It was as if it were the launching pad of greatness. As I stepped up to the podium, I ran my fingers along the wood grains. It felt as though I were touching the embodiment of Christ, my Jesus, the carpenter. With great respect I took a deep breath. It reminded me of those who had stood there before me and behind every other pulpit ever created. It was a place like this that Billy Graham, the greatest Evangelist, and Ravi Zacharias, the greatest apologist, of the world stood. It was behind those pulpits that the pastors from the highest and lowest parts of creation stood. The history of divinity spread amongst the nations behind podiums just like this one.

Although I was standing where so many had stood before, my first words felt futile in my human weakness, but, in Christ, they were bold. I never once lost eye contact with those in front of me. I never lowered my brow in embarrassment as I revealed the intimate secrets of my past. There was no lip biting, labored breathing, and never once did I feel apprehensive. I never tucked my chin in shame. Instead, I stood there and the words of my testimony touched the heart of every person who heard them. I was in Love and it shined from the inside out. There was nothing or no one who could ever put my light beneath a bushel or hide it in a basket. This little light was mine and I was going to let it shine. It was my story. It is my life and it is the only Truth I have ever known.

Right away, I let everyone know I had left my notes at home, but the simplicity of my story was that Jesus Loved Me, and I had no problem sharing that. I went on in some feeble attempt to capture in words what had happened to me since I found Jesus. I explained how it was inevitable that a life born into addiction, abandonment, and abuse would naturally lead to emotional turmoil, abortions, therapy, abusive relationships, multiple suicide attempts, and, ultimately, a life full of self-destructive decisions. After all, I had learned to live my life much like the way an addict would. My mother was an addict, each one of us suffered from her addiction. I am only one of five brothers and sisters. Her addiction molded our personalities, our hurts, habits, and hang ups. From the severe neglect and abuse that I suffered as a child, I developed what is clinically known as Borderline personality disorder.

I went on to explain that Borderline personality disorder (BPD) is a mental and emotional health disorder. Most people who have BPD suffer from problems with regulating emotions and thoughts, impulsive and reckless behaviors, and unstable relationships with other people. People with this disorder also have high rates of co-occurring disorders, such as depression, anxiety disorders, substance abuse, and eating disorders, along with self-harm, suicidal behaviors, and have the highest rates of successful suicides.

Because of this, co-dependency also plagued my relationships. The Webster dictionary defines codependency as a psychological condition or a relationship in which a person is controlled or manipulated by another; I was dependent on the emotions of others which controlled me. This was reflected in my need to have a man who became my god and to serve him without question. I tried to commit suicide more times than I can count. I lost count of the number of abortions that I have had starting at the age of twelve. My emotional roller coaster drove every person I loved away. I gave my first-born child up for adoption and my son, from my first marriage, I sent to live with his father when he was five. I isolated myself from every family member trying to run from a truth that I could not face.

I shared with the congregation my ability to stand there and fill their mind with the horrific images of child abuse and neglect in the worst ways, however, what I thought I would like to share was my journey. I know today, Jesus Loves Me, and He has loved me from the beginning of the earth. He has healed me in places I did not even know I needed healing and continues to do so. He has showed me his great love and mercy. My Jesus loves me so much that there is nothing He won't use to express His love in ways that comfort me and bring me peace. He gives me an opportunity to share His love with the world around me every single day. Although, I have no idea what God has in store for my future or what plans He has laid out before me. I do know this, I know whatever it is, "It is well with my soul."

I stood in front of everyone, as soon as those words left my mouth, I knew it was the end of my testimony. It was so interesting because there was so much more I wanted to say, but I knew it was time to stop. In that moment, at that time, it ended with the final words of the last song the congregation had just sung.

I came down from the pulpit and sat down next to my dad. He put his arm around my shoulder and whispered in my ear, "You just charged the frontlines naked and with a machine gun." What he was telling me is, God had given me a gift to speak, and I was not clothed for battle. My dad had been walking this journey longer than I had, and he knew that I had just waged war against my enemy and war was exactly what was about to pursue me.

After my baptism, my relationship seemed to grow deeper with God. I was always listening and ready to see Him move in my life. I waited with anticipation and every day I asked Him for direction. In my innocence, I was madly in love and wanted to tell the world about Jesus. I couldn't stop sharing what He had done for me. There was a time my tongue swelled up with red sores all over it and it scared me. I thought to myself, "I am never speaking again, I am not telling anyone anything," but the truth is, I couldn't stop. I began to pray to God about what I needed to do and He gave me clear directions.

The first direction He gave me made no sense to me because typically we learn as little children, if the stove is hot, you don't touch it because you will get burned. It was strange that He would put on my heart to find someone to share my story with. Even though I did not agree with him, I went about doing what He asked me to do anyway. I found someone, told them everything, and as soon as I was finished my tongue went back to normal and my faith increased.

That has only happened to me once. There have been a lot of first and last times in my journey with my Father in Heaven who loves me, who is faithful to bring me into complete and total truth. He shows me the same truth that sets me free every single day. I find it in His word, among His people, and in the passing of strangers. There is nothing He won't do to teach me who He is and what He says I am. We live in an eloquent dance of life with one another, learning to be one with Him as Jesus is in Him and He is in Jesus, so am I in them.

God has given me visions; visions that have encouraged the person He is creating me to be. Once I saw myself at the foot of the cross, my eyes intently focused on Jesus' feet nailed to it, my arms lifted in worship as I focused on Him, and sin flew by me without the ability to touch me. I prayed every day for everyone I knew and for the leaders in my church. I have journals filled with the prayers for others. I visited other churches with people who I met. There was this one lady, I just loved her, and she had five children and lived in an apartment off of Palm Beach Ave, a poor area in our city. Her name was Vernestine, I still think about her. She invited me to her church and I was so happy to go with her. It was on a Friday night and our Baptist church only met on Wednesdays and Sundays, so Friday night was good for me.

It was a vibrant church, everyone full of worship, singing aloud, clapping, and full of expressive gratitude. It was fun being there. We stood about five rows from the front and I made sure I was at the end of the isle because I noticed a man sitting in the front pew. He definitely was homeless. You could tell from his clothes, messy hair, and dirty nails. I thought to myself, "I want to share with him," but I couldn't just interrupt service so I waited for it to be over. In our final praise and worship, we all closed our eyes and I began preparing my heart to approach this person I had never met. When I opened my eyes, he was gone.

I dropped my arms to my side, said my goodbyes to my friend and headed for the parking lot. My heart was a little broken. I really wanted to share with him how much Jesus loved him. I got inside my jeep, looked up, and there across the street I saw him. He was bringing his bicycle out from behind the dumpsters. I quickly drove over to where he was and said, "Excuse me, sir, I have something I want to share with you." As he walked over to me, his eyes were an intoxicating blue, and his smile was charming as he looked up to me and said, "Well, I have something I want to share with you." The calmness of his faith settled in my heart. The truth of what he was sharing had a depth I had not yet experienced. He told me he chooses to be homeless to share the love of Jesus with those who are homeless. All I could think of is, "What kind of love is this?"

He wasn't drunk on wine, like I had expected, but he was full of Spirit. He wasn't escaping some horrific tragedy at the bottom of the bottle. He was sharing in the suffering of others with a hope to make a difference. He explained how he gathers food and water from the pantries and shelters to share it with his friends who live in the woods. He wasn't disabled or he definitely did not appear to have any mental health issues. I guess that could be questionable to some, considering he was choosing to be homeless. He told me that the kind of people he helps would not open up to just anyone. They are vagrants living on the out skirts of society and have no desire to do it any other way, but that he was called to bring them hope.

I did not say a word. I could only listen. He shared with me the love of Jesus, told me to have a beautiful night, and rode away on his bicycle. I was baffled by his faith, his loyalty, his wisdom, and for some reason he become symbolic to me. He became a symbol of truth. The truth I found in John 15:13; "Greater love hath no man than this; that a man lay down his life for his friends."

This scripture tells me there is no other love that is greater than the love of one who lays down his life for another. This homeless man, the vagrant living on the outskirts of society, was choosing to lay down his life just like my Jesus laid down His life for me. I am not sure how long I sat in my jeep in the parking lot of that gas station, but I know I cried in amazement of God who sees us all. I am in awe of a creator who is mindful of every single human being alive on earth. In astonishment of a Father who gave His only Son who chose to die and pay the price to give us exactly what God had always intended. I approached him with the hope of sharing the gospel and what he did for me changed my life forever. The impact of his sacrifice keeps me asking myself about the motives of my own heart. I will never forget his story because it plays on repeat in my heart and in my mind. I sat in my jeep and asked God to help me lay my life down to love the same way He loves, so the world will know that He sent Jesus to save us all.

It wasn't long after this encounter that I had decided to fast and pray. I had never done that before, and I got the inkling to try it when I was reading about the shipwreck Paul was in where he said they had not eaten in fourteen days, he then broke bread and gave thanks to God, and shared it with the same people who were going to kill him to prevent his escape. At times, I felt like I had just come through a storm, a shipwreck of my own, and really needed some direction as far as what my next steps were. I did not want to fall into old habits while I was forming new ones. It was important to me to stay close to Jesus, as close as I could, and the only way I knew how to do that was to read His word and follow whatever I could understand.

In those days, I was helping a lot of people; people who I had never met. I had such a hunger to share Jesus with everyone who didn't know him that I sacrificed the relationships with the people who loved me the most. I was always busy doing something for someone else and lacked making time for my sister. The truth is, I

couldn't share the gospel with her, she already knew it. I remember

once, sending her an ultimatum in a letter which she got on her

birthday. Everything about this stinks. I told her I didn't want a

relationship with her until she quit drinking. I told her I planned to

join a group called, "Al-Anon," which could help me understand

how to deal with her alcoholism.

She wrote me back. The amazing part of this story is she burnt my

very unkind and judgmental letter which is exactly what needed to

happen and sent me this:

> *Dear Jennifer, Thanks for writing, how very*
>
> *thoughtful of you. I must tell you it doesn't hurt that you*
>
> *choose to keep your distance. I'm used to it. What does hurt*
>
> *is that someone would or could believe a lie about me. I've*
>
> *done enough without anyone else's help. You see, I recently*
>
> *came to a new understanding that is helping me. Ephesians*
>
> *5:18 and be not drunk with alcohol wine, where in is excess*

but be ye filled with the Spirit. You see being drunk is the world's, i.e satan's, substitute for being filled with the Spirit. I have been in rebellion for twelve years. In [1 John 1-9] if we confess our sins, he is faithful and just to forgive our sins and cleanse us from all unrighteousness. Jennifer, I repent to God and He is just. I will pay for my rebellion, for example, my relationship with you. I don't believe any group will help you understand me. It will however help you understand you and your reaction to me. However, forgiveness is the beginning of healing. I forgive you for not remembering the sacrifices I made for you with God's help. I don't ever have to see you again in this world. I know I'll see you in heaven and we can praise the Lord for eternity together. Know this God will restore everything I've lost tenfold in this lifetime when I look on my Savior's face. Believe what you will, you're going to anyway. I love you and I miss you. Knowing you are saved is worth it. (signed) Karen.

Although I can't remember everything I wrote. I do know it was not a nice letter. I can say now I was taking out my frustrations of my relationship with my mom out on my sister. Before this, I had no idea I wanted my sister to choose me over alcohol and in some way it would be like my mom choosing me over her addiction. I wanted to be important enough to matter. I wanted my sister to pay for my mom choosing her drug of choice over me a million times. I wanted the possibility of my relationship with my mom to be restored in the relationship with my sister.

I stood there holding her letter in my hand while purposeful tears filled my eyes. They came with one purpose, to cleanse my soul from all unrighteousness. Inside my heart was something hidden. What was hidden became visible with each tear drop. Just beneath the surface of despair, I sent her a letter full of anger and grief. Grief at what I had lost with no consideration to what my sister had lost. The evidence of my bitterness was now scrolling down my cheeks and landing on the very letter that broke my heart. Her words broke my heart in a good way. They revealed to me the hardness that I still harbored and triggered the emotions behind my motives which gave me insight into the heart of my letter and the grace she so eloquently displayed over hers.

It is so interesting, that her letter has remained with me all these years. There were times it would float around my house and just show up somewhere. Whenever it does, I always read it and it refreshes my soul every single time. It is a reminder to me that we all have a story that we walk with. It is like the man that I met coming out from behind the dumpster; it is like my mom, who my dad once told me "even crack houses need Jesus" as if to imply she shared Jesus wherever she went, and it is like my sister who struggles with alcoholism. There are things in our life that we will struggle with but those things are not supposed to separate us from our Savior. I cannot run from myself. At my very best I can learn to love myself exactly where I am without allowing my life to dictate my lovability or the lovability of others.

The cross is forever before me, forever behind me, and I am left with only one question. What in the world am I going to do with all the "in-betweens" of my life? If Jesus is my beginning and He is my ending, then He must also be my "everything" in-between. So I ask myself, "How can I do that?" The answer is I can give myself and others the grace we need to grow. The same grace Jesus gives me. He is the faithful one. The one who overcomes, the one who redeems, restores, and replenishes all that is lost. He is the one who has given us His very own Spirit, the Holy Spirit, alive and well, living on the inside of each of us and remains faithful to be our teacher, if we let Him. It is Jesus who carries us into all truth and all knowledge of who He is and the fullness of what He has done.

1 Corinthians Chapter 13 describes to me a love that is full. The fullness of a love that is patient, a love that is kind, a love without envy, one that never boasts, and is not proud, a love that never dishonors others, and is not self-seeking. This is the kind of love that is never easily angered and keeps no records of wrong. A love

that never delights in evil but always rejoices with the truth. It is this love that always protects always trusts, always hopes, and always preservers. It is this kind of love that never fails.

What I know now, I only know in part. What I see now, I see only in part, but when I see Him, face to face, I will know Him fully even as I am fully known, just as the scripture tells me. The truth is, I know nothing, only the cross because it is by the cross, and through the cross, that I have received this kind of love. There is no greater lesson than this one which I have found in 1 Corinthians 13:13 "now, there is three Faith, Hope, and Love. But the greatest of these is love." A love that keeps no records of wrongs, a love that compels me forward onto roads less traveled, giving me joy from the ashes of my past. He has laid down His life for mine and has removed the veil from my eyes to share with me a love worth dying for.

Tino (My Husband), Me,

Elisha (2 yrs) and Cheyanne (8 yrs)

(Bottom Middle)
TJ   David

Chapter Eleven:
He is Faithful

I had just stepped out into the "real world" full of His love and nothing but hope for the future. I knew there were so many in the world that were hurting just like I used to, and I wanted everyone to know what Jesus had done for me He would also do for them. I knew He was no respecter of persons. How could I know that? Because the bible is full of testimonies of all kinds of people from prostitutes to those with leprosy, there were those who waited around thirty-eight years to be healed, and none of that mattered to Him. He spent His life doing what was good and that was exactly what I wanted to do, more than anything else in this world, I wanted to love hurting and broken people.

I had no idea how I would do it, I just knew I wanted to. I wanted to be a reflection of my Jesus; the one who loves me. I wanted so desperately for the world to know the same kind of love that He has given to me. I wanted them to know it was real. It was not some kind of illusion or something I dreamt up to be real. It is tangible. It is life altering. I was not the same. I was never going to

be the same and He was available to anyone who was willing and

to anyone who asks.

The word tells me "who so ever believes in Him shall not perish

but have everlasting life." I know I am a "who so ever" and I know

there are thousands of "who so ever's" passing me every day. I had

been saved from the pit of my destruction and it was the word of

God that accomplished that. Without me reading His word, I would

have never known who He was and what He was like or the depth

of what He had done.

All I knew was I was not going to deny my Jesus. I made it my

mission that everywhere I went Jesus was coming with me. After

all, I had just started studying in 2 Timothy 2:10-13 which says: "If

we died with Him, we will also live with Him." I knew I had died

and wanted to die daily to anything that was not of Him. "If we

endure, we will also reign with Him." I knew I had nothing else to live for, He had become my purpose, and there was nothing greater than learning how to allow Him to "reign" over my life, with the hope that I would one day be a reflection of Him. "If we disown Him, He will also disown us." I knew I could never take the credit for what he had done. I could not deny Him; He is everything to me. "If we are faithless, He remains faithful, for He cannot disown Himself." Faithless, when I am at the end of myself and I have made every wrong decision I could possibly make, I am nothing but grateful because my Redeemer lives and He will never deny me, He will never leave me, He will never forsake me, especially in the middle of the messes that I make.

I was determined to never disown my Savior, and to find those who needed Jesus the most and take hold of their hand in order to connect it with the only hand that saves. I lived everyday looking for someone to share my Jesus with. I learned quickly I never had to look far. They were in the grocery store lines, they were cashiers, pedestrians, co-workers, and, on a really good day, it was family. There is no way possible I can share everything but I want you to know about a few.

She worked as a cashier at the local seven eleven convenience store. She was a bit older, had lost her teeth, and did little to fix herself up. Every day that I saw her, I got to share a little bit more of my Jesus. Sometimes, it started out as just a smile, and it turned in to an encouraging word, and when no one was around a prayer for something that was important to her. Eventually, I gave her my number and invited her to go to the local comedy club with my dad and me. It was something we did on occasion. My dad was a comedian himself, and although, the verbiage could get a bit crude, I loved being there with him.

I picked her up at her home. You never really understand the depth of someone's pain until you see them in their home. She was lost among a mountain of debris with dog feces littering the floor. I had to put Carmex beneath my nose to be able to breathe while we waited to take her and her husband with us. I was saddened by the way she lived and wanted to share with her the beauty of a Savior who had the power to make her life better. I knew part of the problem was that she did not know her value. Somewhere along the way, she had lost sight of her worth and I was determined to be a shining light in her life, unveiling her value and worth.

We laughed together, but mostly I loved watching her and her husband enjoy themselves. We took them home and managed to convince them to come over to our apartment for dinner once. Our friendship didn't last long. At the time, I was not sure why, but since then I have learned that those who God brings into my life are sometimes for a short while, other times for a long while, but only a few last a lifetime. My hope is that she learned a little more about Jesus by knowing me. Not that I am Him, but that I am lead by Him, and that she is loved by Him.

The next person I want to share with you is a girl named Stacy. She was the first friend I made in Florida and I met her at church when I moved here. She was struggling in her relationship at the time and I was like a magnet for the hurting. There was nothing more I wanted to do than to lift the down-trodden because I was there once. I knew Jesus had the comfort they needed and I could be the vessel that could connect them to the "Comforter." We would get together, bible in tow, and go to the club. I would share my testimony with whoever would listen. Most of them were drinking or drunk, but I still believe there were seeds planted in the depths of their souls and God would water them in His timing. His promises are true and correct and when He said, "His Word shall never return void," I believe Him!

We did this for a few months, until, one night it got a little crazy. As we entered the same club we always went to, there was something very different. Everyone looked like they were demonically possessed. If was as if a red flag went up in my spirit telling me to leave immediately. We quickly left and were followed by a man trying to run us off the road welding a knife out

of his window. We pulled into a gas station because we saw an

officer. The crazy man pulled in next to us. We jumped out of the

car and ran to the officer to explain what was happening. The

officer took it from there and we went straight home.

I was young in my faith and my innocence could have gotten me

into a lot of trouble, but God always let me go far enough out onto

a limb before His sovereign grace would pull me back in. I was a

brand new Christian with a heart full of fire ready to spread the

flames of redemption and restoration. The truth is, I wouldn't listen

to wise counsel. It wasn't that I was trying to be rebellious. I was

trying to share Jesus, and lacked the wisdom to know how.

It reminds me of what my dad had told me in the church after my

baptism. I was running towards the front line with a machine gun

in hand completely naked. In other words, I had a story I wanted to

share but I had no idea who I really was in Christ and the depth of that meaning. I just loved Him, I loved Him because He loved me first, and I wanted the world to know His love for them too.

Looking back, I can say I probably scared more people than I helped but that was not my intention. My intention was to share His love with everyone around me. He had changed my life so drastically that I couldn't shut up even if I wanted to. It didn't matter to me if I offended you because Jesus loved you and He had paid a price for you to know it. I am not saying I was right and I am not even saying you have to agree with me, but what I am saying and what I have always said is, "He loves you with an everlasting love."

In those first few months so many things happened, my cousin from Utah, came to stay with us for a while, when he was trying to get clean. My youngest sister and nephew, Taylor, moved to Florida for a change of scenery and to get away from North Carolina. She wanted to start new. My dad was excited about helping her, and I was happy to have her come, but we had no idea

the kind of trouble we were going to get ourselves into. I had a

savior's heart, but the problem was I wasn't the Savior. I thought I

could change the world but what happened was the world ended up

changing me or at least it did for a little while.

My sister struggled with wanting to party and I wanted to share

Jesus. So I thought I would take her to the club, to teach her how to

respect herself and still have a good time. Although she would

always end up being the underage drinker with the "X" on her

hand, holding a beer as high as she could above the crowd, there

was no teaching her. There were probably a few things she could

teach me. I thought it was a good idea to have our dad as our

chauffer. He was happy to do it and we had fun at first. But, I

remember sitting in the back seat of the jeep and watching them in

the front when all of a sudden I felt as though God told me, "She

will make you fall." I shook it off and never said a word. I knew

what the Holy Spirit was trying to share with me and it was simple.

It just meant I could not follow her; I could only try to be an example. It did not change the fact that I had a problem, and the problem was I was having trouble reconciling the world we live in with this new truth that I had been given.

It was a process. I was still looking at circumstances while compromise had been invited into my new walk without me even recognizing it. It would have been safer to stay completely away from the party lifestyle, but instead it drew me in closer. Now keep in mind, God works all things out for His good according to His purpose. I remember sitting on the edge of the bed when suddenly I had an overwhelming desire to go salsa dancing. After all, I did not think that enjoying dancing was bad, as long as I did it alone. I had been doing it for months now and the fact that I wanted to add a little Latino flare was stimulating. I asked around at my job because there were a lot of Latinas who worked there. Once I knew where we would go I talked my sister into joining me. She really was not interested but she went anyway, just to keep me from going alone.

I remember the day clearly. I didn't even know how to speak Spanish. We decided to go to this club called, Junkanoos, on Fort Myers Beach. We played pool for a while. At least, until this guy and his friend came over to our table. When my eyes met with his, I looked away quickly, but definitely noticed he had on loose ripped up jeans with a form-fitting shirt exposing his muscular physique. I couldn't help but notice his honey colored eyes and tan hews of a burnt orange skin tone. He was the most handsome man in all of Florida, I was sure of that, and I knew I was in trouble.

So, I told my sister we had to get out of there, but she was ready to fight to keep her pool table. After all, those were her quarters. It took me a minute but I managed to convince her otherwise. We gave over our pool table and went upstairs. She stayed with me the whole time. There were no disappearing acts at this club, which I thought was a good thing. I never really thought of him anymore that night, but I also did not yet know that every time, from that night forward, when I went to a Spanish club, no matter where it was at; Estero, Naples, Cape Coral, or Fort Myers, he was going to be there.

The guy that made my heart skip a beat and caused butterflies to flip flop inside my belly was everywhere. I didn't want to feel those feelings. I did not want a man in my life ever again. Jesus was my main squeeze and that is how I wanted it forever. So every time I saw him I made sure I stayed on opposite sides of the club until we left.

It was not long before my sister got comfortable enough to start disappearing on me again. So, I spent most of our nights hunting her down. One night, I was looking for her and there he was standing in front of me. He asked me if I wanted a drink, of course, I said, "NO!" But in the same breath I also said, "I only drink water." He got the water, I forgot about my sister, and we danced the rest of the night. Truth is, this would be the man that I would marry, but at that time I had no idea. He didn't speak English, and I didn't speak Spanish, but love is a universal language and eventually we would figure it out because from that night forward we were inseparable.

I found my sister later on that night when we went outside. I remember walking out of the club and going with Tino to his car. That thing was like a beckoning light for my eyeballs. It was a beat-up mess with sun-faded flames plastered across the hood. All I kept thinking the entire time we were walking towards that car was, "that better not be his car." But of course our God has a sense of humor because sure enough that 1994 Toyota Celica was his pride and joy. I found my sister at my car waiting on me and we all went out for breakfast and then went home.

I had decided it was best for me not to ask God about that relationship because I was afraid He would tell me I had to give it up. Therefore, because I wouldn't ask God directly about my new relationship, He gave me visions instead. One morning, I was praying and I saw myself looking at Jesus. There was light all around me but my iron-clad focus was on Christ. Nothing could come between me and my focus on Him. In the vision, I saw a figure to the right. He was far away, and although I would not take my eyes off of Jesus, I was mindful of the person's movement towards me. This person walked straight up to me, but I never turned to look at him, I only focused on Christ before me. The image of the man stood next to me and turned to see what I was focused on. The man then joined me and we focused on Christ together.

Although God had given me a vision, I failed miserably at following it. This new man in my life, Tino, had most of my attention. I mean, he didn't have my Morning Prayer time because we didn't live together, but he had all of my spare time. I spent four months compromising with his lifestyle. By November, I joined him. I started drinking and partying the same way he did. My reasons for going to the club had changed. I no longer went to share Jesus with a broken and dying world and I found myself completely enamored by this beautiful person beside me. I was in love and I knew it the moment he shared the story of when he was a boy in Honduras. He told me he created toy men out of sticks and oranges and I found him endearing.

He was kind and gentle. He never once raised his voice and opened my doors all the time. He never touched me in a demeaning way or treated me like I was somehow less than him. He made me feel loved, beautiful, and when I was with him, I felt as though he crowned me as his queen, giving me his full attention. We laughed at the same things, even though, we struggled to communicate. It was six months before we communicated well, but it was worth it to me.

During that time, my dad wanted nothing more than to preserve my Christianity. I had been set apart for Jesus not for some illegal, non-papered Latino trying to become a citizen, which was not true.

He had his green card already, but my dad was angry. He had just witnessed God rescue me from a horrible abusive relationship. He had just seen me travel across country and was a witness to the amazing transformation God had made inside my heart.

Once when we pulled into the drive way, my dad was sitting in his favorite place in the garage with the door opened. By now his back issues had gotten much worse and he was half bent over. On that night, what he had to say to both of us was important enough for him to make it to his feet and walk to the jeep. He was half bent over carrying his bible with him. He held it straight in the air and yelled at Tino. He said, "Do you see that girl right there? She is a Jesus girl and you may have her now but she is coming back." He pointed to me with his bible and said, "She Loves Jesus," and walked away.

It was obvious that I needed to go inside and have a talk with my dad. We said goodnight to each other and I went inside the apartment. My dad confronted me with what I was doing. I will never forget what I said and what he said back to me. I told him that this is how "the world is" and his only response was. "Exactly." It took a few years to actually understand the depth of what he had said that night. He was right. I was behaving like the world behaves not like someone who had been transformed by the most amazing love ever given to mankind.

That night, my dad warned me that I would be pregnant by November and, sure enough, nine months later in August of 2007, I gave birth to a baby girl that we named Elisabeth Cheyanne. Elisabeth meaning God's promise and Cheyanne meaning two united nations. God had given me her name on the way into a restaurant the day I told my oldest sister of my pregnancy. Her name, "Cheyanne," was written across the pavement in chalk on the sidewalk in front of the entrance door where we ate. I also saw it when we left that restaurant. It was written on the back of a truck inside of a heart. I was convinced "Cheyanne" was her name and my husband named her Elisabeth. Together her name means God's promise to unite nations and that was exactly what she was. She

was a combination of two nations unified in the promise of God's

love.

I knew names were important and she was important to me, but a

lot happened in nine months. I left my apartment that I shared with

my dad. Tino and I moved three times within those months, I lost

my job, and my car was repossessed, which I had never

experienced before. I was four months pregnant when I told Tino I

was never going back to a club. It was hard to let him make his

own choices and I cried almost every single day. I had given him

an option to leave us. I told him I would not go after him for child

support that my God would take care of us. If he did not want this

family then I would be okay, but I could not live the way we were

living anymore.

In those days, I was my worst enemy. I spent a lot of time thinking

God was disappointed in me, that maybe He was mad at me for the decisions I had made. But my thoughts never lined up with His

word and God's actions only smothered me with love all the more.

In the middle of my mess, I never stopped praying, I never stopped

reading His Word, and I never stopped worshipping Him. As a

matter of fact, it made me seek Him more and I learned there was

nothing I could do that would take away from what Jesus had

already done for me.

However, when I was pregnant, I was full of condemnation. The

truth was I didn't need anyone else to condemn me, because I was

pretty good at doing that all by myself. Even though I was

suffering from condemning myself, it did not stop me from

praising and worshiping God. Every day Tino left for work, I put

my music on, I danced, and I rubbed my belly, praising God for

this unborn child. I had not been happy about a baby being inside

my womb for years and it made me rejoice all the more. The truth

is, all but two of my past pregnancies came with feelings of doom

and despair because I knew they had only one fate; they had no

choice; they lived and died inside my amniotic fluid. So it was easy to fall in love with God's beautiful living creation inside of me. I loved everything about being pregnant. I was a proud mommy and no one could take that from me. I loved her with every ounce of my being and I was not ashamed of her, but I was grossly ashamed of my circumstances.

But all I could think of was how far I had fallen. I wanted to become what Jesus would have me be but instead I arrived a year later, in the parking lot of my first church, as an unwed pregnant mother. It was strange because even though I was pregnant and I felt bad for not being married, I still loved my daughter and thought of her dad like he was the only man I ever loved. The truth is, he is the only man I ever had the ability to love because when I met him, I had been made whole by Jesus. He did not get the scattered me, or the broken me. He got "the whole me," the one that was full of joy, full of love, full of self-value and worth. Tino did not have the ability to make me whole because my wholeness came directly from my relationship with Jesus. Tino could not "add" to me when it came to my value or even my happiness, only

Jesus could do that. Therefore, there was nothing Tino could do that would steal, kill, or destroy me. Instead, God gave me the grace I needed to see the very best in him and to look past his flaws into the future of his full potential.

I spent a lot of time feeling bad about not being married. So I did the only thing I knew to do. I ran to my Estero church. I had some questions and needed some answers. When I arrived to my church, I got out of this beat up old 1994 Toyota Celica. Yes, that same car that I desperately hated became the only vehicle we had for about three years. It not only provided us transportation but I used it to help others. I constantly told them, "This car runs on faith and fuel." Isn't it just like God to make me grateful for the very car I hated when I first saw it. He is amazing like that!

I remember talking with the church's secretary. She was from North Carolina and I thought she was the most beautifully elegant woman I had ever met. I used to call her my southern belle; she was stunning, full of grace, respectful, polite, well-kept, and her

alluring southern accent made me feel like I was at home. I stood

there waiting for her to invite me in and when she did my heart

poured out to her. I explained everything to her and then she asked

me a question. The question was, "Do you love him like he is your

husband?" I said, "Yes, I see him as my husband because he is the

first person I have ever loved from a place of wholeness." Her

response was priceless, she said in the most wonderfully

enchanting southern accent, "Well, Jennifer, I don't think Adam

and Eve had any marriage papers. I believe God is a God who

knows our hearts and if he is your husband in your heart then that

is between you and God."

Those words were the sweetest words I had ever heard. The ease

with which she spoke lifted the weight of condemnation off of my

entire pregnancy. In that moment, I realized although pregnancy

was a consequence of my actions it was not a badge of dishonor.

My consequences did not have the power to dictate condemnation

into my heart. My circumstances were not greater than God's truth and God's truth says in Romans 8:1, "There is no condemnation for those who belong to Christ Jesus." By now, if I knew anything, I knew I belonged to Christ Jesus and there was nothing I could do to change that. My God knew me and I knew Him; He knew my heart, and that was good enough for me.

I left the church full of zeal and started a new project. I was famous for new projects. Constantly starting them but rarely finishing, but this time I had found a new determination. The door of the fiery furnace of condemnation had been opened and I was coming out of it not even smelling of the flames. I had one resolve, to share with the world the beauty of my pregnancy and the pain abortion had caused me. I spent the final months of my pregnancy doing just that. I had created a brochure, printed it out, and loaded it on disks. I then went to every church I knew and a left a copy of the brochure and the disk with them in case they wanted to share it with their youth group. I don't know if anyone ever did but what I do know is I no longer carried condemnation with me. I was finally free to hold my head high, pregnant and all, allowing His glory to shine through me.

I no longer spent the days before our daughter was born crying, begging God to forgive me. I now knew His faithfulness to forgive me had come from the cross. I did not have to earn it. It was already mine. Instead, I spent those days sharing the message He put inside my heart and praising His beautiful name. I was elated when the time came to give birth to our beautiful little girl. The doctor had scheduled me to induce labor and it was time to go. I had spent nine months watching my belly grow. I loved her the moment I knew she was there inside of me. When I heard her heart beat for the first time, I cried. I cried because I knew I was carrying a tiny little soul inside of me. It changed me and I was so grateful for how far God had brought me. The truth is, I didn't even know what I had missed out on until I got the chance to "feel it" for myself.

That day my sister met us at the hospital. I wanted her with me during this amazing time. It was not long after we arrived that Elisabeth Cheyanne was born. I had never felt more connected to another human being in all of my life, and, for the first time, I understood the pain behind the inescapable truth of abortion. The cries I cried, from every single abortionist's table, come from the bottomless pit of a mother's love. A love I had never experienced before, not from my mother or from any other birth of a child. This is not to say I did not love my other two children because I did. I loved them the best way I knew how, but I loved them from a very broken place; a place that had never experienced what it was like to be connected to another human being. I spent my life being disconnected and consumed by my own pain. I did not have the ability to love them the way they deserved to be loved, until now. I cried for every single little baby that had been torn from my womb, I cried for the child I gave up for adoption, and I cried for my son, the one who got the weekend/holiday mom.

I wept for all that was lost, but I also wept for what I had gained through the birth of my first born; after being born again myself. I had been made whole. I understood what love was. There is no greater love than the love I had found in the fullness of Christ laying His life down for mine. He laid His life down for the hope that I might come to know that same kind of love and here I was staring back at her in my arms, understanding the fullness of His love for us.

I couldn't love her more because I had been made to love through Christ. I was overwhelmed by the immense joy that filled my heart. My little girl, my Cheyanne, our daughter together, Tino bent over me to hold her little hand, and a tear fell from his eye as he lifted her from my arms. He held her up to heaven. Right there in the middle of everyone, Tino dedicated Cheyanne to God and promised her to be faithful to God as He raised her in His love.

When we left the hospital, neither one of us knew, the battle had just begun. The war had been waged and only time could tell the outcome. After her birth, I returned to the hospital in order to have a surgery, and hemorrhaged within the first week. God's timing is impeccable because my sister and her husband were on a sobriety binge and had been sober for a few months. It was perfect timing because she was able to help us with Cheyanne while I was hospitalized and Tino worked.

Tino continued to struggle, even after our daughter's birth, he struggled with himself and with God. He wasn't sure of a lot of things, one being marrying me. He didn't know if Jesus would approve of him marrying me since he had been through a divorce. As a matter of fact, he wasn't sure Jesus approved of him at all because of all that he was doing. The intensity of the war between his flesh and spirit made him doubt, but God remained faithful through it all.

As a witness, I knew there were a lot of things that God spoke into Tino's life long before he was my husband, and there were a lot of things He had yet to speak. Tino told me of a vision he had once when he lived in Texas of girl with light hair, hiding in a basement full of graves. He didn't realize what he was seeing until after I had the ability to share my testimony with him. When he heard about the abortions I had, he understood his vision. God had gone before me to prepare his heart to accept me just the way I was. In that moment, God revealed to him that it was me he saw in the vision. Tino understood that it was God who planted the seed of compassion, for the girl in the basement with the graves, inside his heart.

God has a way of being faithful to His plans, even if we are completely unaware of them. Neither one of us knew it was God who moved us from our states and into Florida around the same time. When we met each other, there was an instant connection, and we both knew we had no plans of being with anyone else, but it took a while to push the world out from between the two of us.

The world had captivated Tino's soul, but his heart remained with God. He wasn't happy in the world. He longed for something more. He wanted his family but struggled with his flesh.

But he wasn't the only one struggling, I remember us going out on a boat with my sister after the birth of our daughter Cheyanne. I got wasted on alcohol, but I got wasted because I was sad. I was sad for a few reasons. I kind of figured, "if you can't beat, them you might as well join them," but it grieved my soul. Let me explain why. I had gotten used to my sister being sober and enjoyed our relationship together, but she started drinking again and I felt like I lost her. I was angry at God. I knew she used Him to get sober and I felt like she had thrown God away when she was done. The key word being "I" because now I know she has her own personal relationship with our Father, and He is big enough to handle all of our humanness.

Including my own; I can hardly believe I shook my fist at heaven and said, "How can You let her use You like that?" His response came quickly. He put me in my place by saying, "The great "I AM" is a usable God and when my children call on me, I answer them." Of course, I recoiled on the inside. His voice made me feel small, yet lifted me at the same time to a higher level of understanding. I asked Him for forgiveness but it didn't take away my feelings of loss. Another reason for "joining them" was I felt frustrated about Tino. I thought for sure after Cheyanne's birth he would stop drinking and clubbing, but he didn't. He spent the money we had on what he wanted and not on what we needed. I knew he was not changing and now we had a daughter together. I didn't want to lose my family but I also knew we couldn't keep going on the way we were.

Later that evening, we returned from boating. My niece was babysitting Cheyanne. I was thankful for that because I was so sick. I was sick the entire night. I remember sitting on the edge of their pull out bed and praying for it to go away. God spoke to my heart. To think He was especially mindful of me even in the middle of my mess is sometimes unbelievable. He told me to look at myself and He asked me if this is how I wanted to live for the rest of my life. It scared me sober. His voice has a tendency to that. It had the ability to rise up from the depths of my soul. In a soft quiet whisper that is always loud enough to penetrate the darkness and stun me into obedience. Not like an "I'm going to whip you" obedience but more like an "if this is what you really want, I am about to let you have it" kind of obedience. I made a decision, right then, that there was no way I was ever going to drink again. I did not want to live that way.

I woke up later that day knowing something had to change. So, I just told God I was ready for whatever He wanted to do. It wasn't long after that God asked me to leave Tino. I cried. I was devastated, but I packed my things and moved in with a friend and her mother. I knew it was God who had endowed me with grace and given me the strength to make the best choice for my daughter and me. I had to walk away. I had to let God deal with Tino on His own; without "my" intervention. The truth was, the only course of action I knew how to take was to "beat him over the head with the bible" and that clearly wasn't working. I had to let God reveal to him the truth behind the choices he was making in his life and how they could destroy his future.

It was true he was struggling with the desire to have all that the world says is good, like alcohol. As crazy as this sounds, none of his actions stopped me from believing in the man I knew he could be. I knew he loved Jesus. He expressed it not only in his words but also in his actions towards me. I mean, one of our first dates was us sitting on the rocks by the river, while he strummed his guitar, and we sang the universal song, "Hallelujah." I knew Tino loved Jesus but I did not know how to bring him back to Jesus. I couldn't force Tino to allow Jesus to reign over his life again, but that never stopped me from trying, and failing miserably. I knew why I had to leave and I believe it had more to do with me than it did with him.

I had no job. I had no money, but He made a way out for me. If there is one thing I have learned, it is that when God asks you to do something, He always provides a way. It is our job to know Him, so that when He guides, we follow and, the truth is, He makes Himself known to us. It is never a guessing game. God is very clear and the only mouth piece He needs is a willing heart. While I stayed with my friend and her mother, we became very close. I was thankful that her mother loved Jesus like I did. We spent a lot of time together studying the word, praying, and fasting in the days and months following. I had received clear instruction from God. I was only to go with Tino when he invited me to go to the church.

I was excited to share with Tino what I had recently learned from my dad. I told him that my church in Estero now had a Spanish service, but weeks passed before he ever invited us and when he did, I said no. I said no because by then, my friends had convinced me not to get back together with him. I was clearly torn, because I wanted my family unit together. I did not want my baby girl

coming from a broken home. I wanted the very best for her. I never

wanted her to suffer the way I did. I wanted her to have her daddy

and I wanted us to be a family. The truth was, they had helped me

so much and I felt like I owed them in some way. Not because they

made me feel that way, they didn't. It was my own internal

struggle. In other words, I had a hard time trying to please

everyone. It actually took Tino telling me he was leaving Florida

before I would change my ways and become obedient to God's

direction. When he said he was leaving, all I could hear in my head

was what God had asked me to do, and I knew I had not been

doing it. I also knew there was a good possibility that I was about

to lose my family and all that I had prayed for, all because I

wanted to please everyone.

I asked him why he wanted to leave. He said it was because he had

lost what was important. After that conversation, I begged God for

another chance. I promised God I would obey Him, above my

friends, even if that meant I would lose them and a place to stay.

The truth was, my Father in Heaven wanted my family together. He wanted to give me my heart's desire and I almost lost it. I almost lost it because I was too concerned about someone else and what they thought. Once again, I found myself begging God for forgiveness. I prayed for another chance to say yes to His directions and not to those around me, and He was faithful to give it to me. God heard me and answered my prayers. I know He is the faithful One, not me. He was the one who prompted Tino to try one last time and when he called again, I said yes.

And as I said yes, I understood I was standing on the promises of God. I knew that if I would obey Him, then He would work it all out for our good. I knew that even though I had been faithless to follow His directions before, I was never out of His reach. He never lost sight of me. He would be with me through it all. I knew I didn't have all the answers, but I knew the One who did. It is Him who is faithful to teach me in every way, no matter what path I take and I knew the Holy Spirit was strong enough to help us handle our difficulties. I knew He would never flutter away at the first sign of our problems.

I understood if I died with Him, I would also live with Him. In other words if I can learn to lose sight of myself and die daily to what I think, feel, and want, and follow His directions then I will really live. I will experience the abundant life He has promised me. If I endure through the process of letting go then I will reign with Him, I will get to share in His glory, but if I choose not to let Him lead me, therefore denying Him, then I am also denying the possibility of all of His promises to reign in my life. If I could learn to do all of this, then our family would have a chance, a chance for a hope and a future together in Christ because it is Him who is the redeemer and the restorer of life. I knew He would be faithful to my husband to help him find his way and I knew He would be faithful to me, to help me find mine.

Chapter Twelve:

I Am Forgiven

After saying yes to go to church with Tino, there was a little bit of tension in the home. I am not sure if it was coming from me or from my friends, but I knew the grace that was over me to stay was gone and that I would need to move out. The truth is, Tino was ready for us to come back. He had been asking me for a few weeks, but I told him he had to marry me first. We spoke to the pastor of our little Spanish church who gave us a hundred dollars to pay for the cost to get married. I dragged Tino to the courthouse, with baby Cheyanne in tow, we said our vows, signed the paperwork, and moved back home.

The day we arrived at our tiny little trailer was full of joy but it was also hard. I cried for a week because of the condition it was in. It was horrible. The floors were falling in; I could see the ground outside from the shower. The kitchen sink sat in an old box made of plywood that was eaten up by termites and there were holes in the bottom of the walls shaped like mouse houses. At night, the termites swarmed inside the trailer, their wings fell off, and they crawled around wherever they fell. I was relieved I had a mosquito net to cover us when we slept. So yeah, I cried for a week, and then I put my big girl pants on and started doing the best with what I had.

We also continued going to church together with baby Cheyanne in tow. This would be the same place I would learn one of the greatest lessons of my faith, but it was also the place where my husband Tino and I would serve, worship, and grow together. The Spanish services were being held inside the Baptist church on evenings when they did not have service. I was thankful that God had given us a place to grow but I did not know enough Spanish to understand the teachings thoroughly, and so I spent my evenings reading the scriptures they were reading from and taking notes of my own. The more time we spent in the church, the more I understood the language and the more I wanted to share what God was showing me.

I was so desperate for someone to listen to the beauty I was discovering in the scriptures that I came across more like a "Jack Russell" dog bouncing around its owner begging for attention. Of course, I can see that now but then I was just excited and full of zeal for my Savior. I was determined to share with them what God was sharing with me, but mostly I think I may have undermined the pastor's wife unintentionally. At the time, I had no idea about the importance of "position" in church. Like whose name went where and who was responsible for what. I had no back-ground so how in the world was I going to know there was this "unspoken" chain of command.

I just wanted to help people and I wanted to help the church. So, I volunteered. I volunteered to be the secretary, although, we were still riding on faith and fumes, I knew God would provide the money for the gas to get back and forth. They allowed me to take that position because they needed help with applying for their 501c3, which is the financial status the IRS needed to be an official church. It enabled them to accept donations and not pay taxes, among other things.

I did my research, wrote the plan to meet with the criteria required by the IRS, created their by-laws, incorporated them, and opened the bank account for the church. It took several months to finish. At the same time, we were learning in the church. I learned about spiritual war-fare, mostly. That was a pretty big thing apparently. I had not heard so much about demonic possession and deliverance in all my life. I guess that is what they focused on mostly. I am not sure because I didn't understand everything they were saying. I just kept my head in the bible, studied while I was in church, and prayed with the church.

They made me feel like we were a part of a family and I wanted so badly to be accepted by them. They collected promised donations and held you accountable for those donations. We had monthly meetings and spent a lot of time arguing about whether the church should supply water bottles or not. Sometimes, it got annoying but I was happy to have been named a "director" in the church, not that I really understood what that was, but I was it.

Being a director, I had gone to the pastor's wife and talked to her about a conference that I felt like God had put in my heart. It was going to be called "the Invitation." I wanted it set up like a wedding. At the time, I had a job as a wedding designer for a local company. We did not have much money but the wedding designer promised to do the flowers for free. The pastor's wife agreed to invite some of the people from other churches that we visited, which was a big thing in the Spanish community. It was normal to visit other churches on special events like when a "Prophet" would come into town or Encounters. An encounter was like a conference but it lasted three days. There was no contact from the outside world and no cell phones allowed. I had never seen anything like that before. Prior to the Spanish church, the only thing I had been to was a bible study, dinner, maybe a BBQ, or a yard sale at the church but nothing like an Encounter.

The first encounter I had ever gone to was hosted by a church called Ministerio De Banderas De Cristo, my husband loved that church, and that encounter made a huge difference in our life. It was the place where they washed my feet and made me feel accepted. It was the place where I danced to praise and worship music without any regard to those around me. I danced as if I were dancing to my King in heavenly places. We spent three days there together, my husband and I, they rekindled our love for Jesus and sparked the flame inside our hearts to serve as One, together before Christ. It was beautiful and I could never take away from what we gained during those three days. But not every encounter is the same and neither is every church.

At the time that I approached the pastor's wife, I wasn't asking to host an encounter. I just wanted to host this very small two-hundred person conference that lasted only a few hours on a Saturday afternoon. I shared everything that I had done and she seemed to accept it and wanted to help with the invitations. I had

spent several months preparing. Using the little money I had to

print brochures, tickets, and develop the material for the

conference. The day of the event I learned the pastor's wife did not

do what she told me she would do. She invited no one. The

wedding designer delivered the flowers. They looked like leftovers

from a week old wedding. Nothing was going like I had planned. I

had spent so much time invested in this conference and thought I

had the support of those who were helping me.

I went to the front of the church and lay on the steps of the altar.

The same alter I had given my testimony at after my baptism and I

cried. My friend came to the altar and laid the bible out in front of

me. Opened to this scripture; "Though there are no sheep in the

pen and no cattle in the stalls, yet I will rejoice in the Lord, I will

be joyful in God my Savior" Habakkuk 3: 17-18. I read those

words, looked up, and there she was. My friend, she was the one

who gave me all those clothes for Cheyanne. The same person who

would, without hesitation, pop a squat with me, in the middle of the floor in a department store, to share in His Word. She knew me

before I was pregnant, when I was first in love with Jesus, no

matter where I went I was ready to share and now here she was

sharing with me. I got to my feet, turned around, and was surprised

by all of those who showed up in spite of everything. One by one,

all of the people that I had jumped around like a "Jack Russell"

filled the pews. All of the ones that would come to my home to

have coffee and study with me were there. Every person that I

spoke life into filled those pews. It was nowhere near two hundred

people but every person that was supposed to be there showed up.

They were there to support me, and although I'll never know if

anything I shared helped them, I know one thing, God's Word will

never return void and I trust and believe in that.

After it was over, the pastor's wife approached me. She told me I

needed to learn a lesson. I needed to learn I cannot do anything by

myself. It was not my place. In other words, I had stepped over

some invisible boundary that I was unaware of. In the moment, all

I could think of was how terrible I felt. I trusted her. It wasn't the fact that she betrayed me but that she did it on purpose. It hurt me but I had no idea where this would eventually lead.

The pastor's wife was my leader. I accepted her as that, but there are a few things I think I need to explain before we go any further. The church Tino and I attended was housed in the Estero Baptist church but it was not a part of that church. The church we were in attended the Encounters hosted by Ministerio de Banderas de Cristo, and claimed to be under their umbrella of spiritual covering, but was not. It was a small church with leaders that answered to no one but themselves. At the time, I did not understand anything; I just accepted all they told me as "gospel." I often thought they must know better; they are the leaders of the church. I mean, we were told, more times than I can count, obedience brings blessings and the Lord knew we were in need of His blessings. So, we became their obedient little followers. We fasted when they told us to, we gave them money when they asked, and when they said it was time to go to an encounter, we went.

Eventually, because I did not have the ability to keep quiet, the time came that the pastor of Ministerios de Banderas de Cristo invited me to speak at the next encounter. It was not my first time. Anytime any-one handed me the microphone, it was going to be a minute because I had things to say. There was nothing that gave me more joy than to share what Jesus had done for me, and to let everyone know, what He did for me He will do for anyone who is willing.

I stood in front of a few hundred people and shared what God had done inside of me. It was amazing. I got to pray for them. Dance with them. I got to love on them and, so far, there was nothing greater than that moment, but when I got home I had an overwhelming feeling of fear. I did not understand it, so I put on praise and worship music and refused to turn it off. The next day I thought it was a good idea to contact the pastor's wife. After all, she was my leader. I let her know what was happening and she told me she would get back to me.

This is when, for the first time, confusion had entered into my walk with Christ. I had invited her into a position of authority over me without even realizing it. I sought after her advice before I sought after God's. At the time, I thought she knew better than me because she knew how to deal with this "demon" business. It took her one week to destroy my testimony. In one week, she had convinced everyone I knew that I was possessed with twenty-three demons. All of which had taken possession of me through my past. Every childhood abuse I had suffered from had opened a door into my current life. In one week, she had thrown a-way every single item that was in my tiny trailer that she felt was demonically possessed. Every piece of clothing that came from Good-will (which is where I shopped mostly). Every piece of jewelry I had from my past. Everything of value was gone and anything that looked pretty was thrown away. It was all possessed. At the time, I really did not know and I thought to myself, "Well, if it's possessed, then I don't want it anyway." If it had a demon, throw it away. In the end, none of that helped because, according to them, I could never be clean; I was the possessed one.

I was completely confused; it made no sense to me because everything I had ever studied told me that ALL things had passed away and ALL things had been made new. Not according to the pastor's wife, who apparently was now leading the church in rebuking demons, and she had become the lead authority. I was told I could not speak to anyone because I might pass my demons on to them and they could not speak to me. The entire church was told to speak in tongues when I spoke in order to protect themselves from the demons I was spreading. Needless to say, I obeyed because obedience brings blessings. I was sat in the back of church and could not participate with the others. My heart was broken.

Apparently, my husband needed a break because out of the blue he decided we were taking a trip to Texas. My oldest sister had recently left Florida and moved there so I wanted to see her anyway. The pastor's wife advised me not to go, but my husband used his authority and told her I was going, which I was happy to oblige. When we got there, Tino's sister's church invited me to share my testimony. I called the pastor's wife and asked her if it was okay; she told me no. By this time, I was really confused; my skepticism had grown leaps and bounds because all the while I have been studying the word and what God says about me. I had been shunned and cast out by the church, not allowed to participate with others, so there was only one place I was getting my truth. I no longer listened to the church. I was reading the Word and everything she was saying was contradicting what Jesus was showing me. How could I not share what Jesus had done in my life.

I shared with my sister what had happened to me. She couldn't believe it and she was so sorry for everything I had gone through.

She told me to never let anyone stop me from sharing my Jesus. So that is what I did. I went to the church and did exactly what filled my heart with joy the most. I shared my Jesus, and when I was done, Tino's sister told me that where ever I go, God will open the doors for me. I learned a valuable lesson that night. I was reminded of the time my tongue had swollen, and the Holy Spirit revealed to me to find someone to share Jesus with, and when I did, it went away. At the time, I had just shared my Jesus with a group of people and had absolutely no fear because this is what I knew, the scriptures say, "Perfect Love Casts Out All Fear" 1 John 4:18.

I was not afraid anymore. I knew who my Jesus was and no one was going to change the gospel truth that had set me free. If I was afraid, I would trust God who cares for me, the One who says the righteous will not be shaken. I was not going to be shaken from the only truth that ever set me free. The shackles of my past had been removed, dealt with by the cross. I was no longer in chains and when the Word tells me I have been set free, I believe it. There was only one problem, the enemy needed me to shut up. My faith was

shaking the ground he stood on and this was not a problem for me,
because once again the TRUTH had set me free.

The Word has told me, again and again, that there is one gospel
truth. I have been betrothed to one husband, promised to one
savior, and I am a pure virgin being presented to Christ. The virgin
of One Word, the Word that does not contradict the gospel I have
received, the gospel that has been taught to me by His word in a
personal relationship with Him. I have received one Spirit, the
Holy Spirit, not the spirit of some gospel that keeps me bound in
chains to a past that has been nailed to the cross. In the scriptures
Paul warns me of the potential of accepting a different gospel, he
warns me of being led astray by another gospel, different from the
one I know to be true. The scripture tells me in 2 Corinthian 11: 4
For [you seem willing to allow it] if one comes to you and
preaches a Jesus other than the Jesus we preached, or if you
receive a different spirit from the Spirit you received, or a different
gospel from the one you accepted, you tolerate all of this
beautifully [welcoming deception]. The interesting part of being

deceived is, you do not know you are being deceived. I was in the church. I had a pure heart. I was beguiled by the cunning tongue of God's Word being used to manipulate His people. Unwittingly, I was being led away from the simplicity of my sincere and pure devotion to Christ. This happened to me, a different gospel had been shared with me and it happened in the church, but it no longer had power over me.

On our return home, the pastor's wife called me and invited me to another encounter, but this encounter was with a different church. I got off the phone with her and prayed. I told God I wanted to go with her, but I wanted Him to show me the Truth, His Truth, as He saw it. I called her back to tell her I was going. She then informed me to pack my bags that we would be leaving the next day.

I was gone three days but I am going to summarize these three days in the lessons that God shared with me there. The first lesson I found was in the first session at the encounter. There were probably about fifty people on this trip, maybe more. We were packed into a small room. The lady in the front spent forty-five minutes talking about the pain in her childhood and about five minutes on Jesus. She then instructed everyone to get on their knees and rebuke the demons from their childhood. I obeyed in as much as I could. I knelt down; I lifted my hands, and started praising God for all that He had rescued me from. I was not loud or disruptive; I quietly praised Jesus for making me new when the leader of the conference came over to me. She asked me what I was doing. I told her and she told me, "Now is not a time to praise God, now is a time to rebuke demons." Immediately, what I felt in my heart was I will never find a place in God's Word that tells me that demons have a position above my Father in Heaven. I knew I had the authority to praise God at ALL times. I continued praising God until they were finished.

I went back to my bunk marked by an "X." I was officially cast as the demonically possessed for the next three days. Away from everyone that loved me, no phone, and no way to leave, I was stuck, but I was not alone. God was with me the entire time. He led

me and instructed me over the next three days. I didn't always

understand the depth of what He had me do but I was obedient to

Him and not to them. Once, they had us go to the front to shake a

basket over our head, which was to represent the blessings that I

received at this encounter, but what God had me do was shake the

basket over the conference leader's head. When I did, she said,

"Wow, I'll receive your blessings." And I thought, "You can have

ALL that comes from this encounter, but you can never take what

my Father has given to me." Another time, they surrounded me

with their backs toward me while they sang and danced to the

song, "Get Behind Me Satan," as if I were him. I also got to give

an offering; God gave me the perfect scripture as I sat there

waiting for my turn. I wrote on a note these words from John 18:23

"If I have said anything wrong, make a formal statement about the

wrong, but if I spoke properly, why do you strike me?"

While I was there, I never stopped sharing God's goodness, my

testimony, or about my amazing Jesus. I just couldn't be quiet but at the same time I was not disruptive or disrespectful. I want no part of destroying any measure of faith in the body of Christ because I love Him. I was not going to be used as a tool to squash the heart of anyone else. That is not say it was easy because there were times during those three days it got to be unbearable. The truth is, God uses people, all kinds of people, from all kinds of different lifestyles, and walks of life, and in all kinds of situations. The truth is no matter what church you are going to, if God wants to use you, He will. Just like the few people He used to encourage me during the hardest times of those three days. I even got to sneak away from the group and be alone for a minute, and I needed it. On our way to breakfast, I was able to slip behind the building and sit with my Father. I needed His love. I needed to feel His love. I had been shunned, rejected, cast out, turned away, and all because I loved Jesus. All because I stood up for the only truth that I knew and I refused to accept a different gospel.

I couldn't wait to get on that bus and go home. As we drove down the highway, a young mother sat beside me. She told me how tired she was and I knew why; during these three days there is no

sleeping. So she asked if I would sit next to her to keep them from

waking her up while she tried to sleep because she was going home

to a newborn and had to be at work the next day. I did what she

asked but they still bothered her. At one point, people were

hanging their heads out of the windows screaming. There was so

much disorder on the bus, people jumping, screaming, dancing,

and falling over, and when we arrived at the church, they had a

celebration waiting for everyone.

Not for me, I wanted to leave. I got off the bus and was looking for

Tino and Cheyanne. I found the car but they were waiting inside.

So I went to go find them, and when I did, I begged Tino to take

me home, but he wouldn't. I know why. He expected me to share

the amazing things that happened at the encounter, but this

encounter was not like the last one. I asked him for the keys to the

car so I could wait outside. He gave them to me with a puzzled

look on his face. I couldn't get to the car fast enough and as soon

as I did, tears welled up from deep inside of me. They filled my eyes as the dam of emotions exploded; the tears cascaded down my cheeks. Everything that had been suppressed for three days fell out of me. I had been crucified in the sense of the unmerited criticism, and the unrelenting claws of bitterness that had scraped across my soul and I had never felt so attacked in all of my life. This was no pain like this one. I had never experienced this before. I moaned in anguish over being crucified by the very people who were supposed to love me. The ones who had been called to build me up had just spent three days of unrelenting attempts to tear me down piece by piece.

It wasn't long before Tino returned to the car with Cheyanne. I was so happy to see him but couldn't explain all that I had just been through. He tried to talk me into staying, but he knew I couldn't. He didn't know why but I was in no shape to go back inside. We went home and didn't speak about what happened again, but he knew something was wrong because I refused to go back to that church. Eventually, after about a week, he convinced me to go to our leaders meeting. I told him it was not a good idea but I did it for him. By this time, I knew the truth and I was angry about the "gospel" they were sharing. That meeting ended with me heaving the bible in the air, and chanting "The bible is all truth." I told the pastor's wife to throw away her demonic books and that God's Word was all she needed. I told her if it is not in God's Word then she hasn't any business sharing it. Eventually, she told me I would always have a "hair in my soup," which is apparently a Spanish saying. In other words, I would never be clean, which I knew was a lie.

It took six months for God to destroy that church. I say it was Him, not because of me but because of His truth. The same woman who told me I would always have "a hair in my soup" was the same woman who would come knocking on my door months later to tell me she knew God loved me and that I loved God. She also told me of the suffering the church was going through. All the leaders had lost their jobs, moved out of the state, and the pastor had been deported. They tried to keep it going but it didn't work out. The church was destroyed in six months from the day of that weekend encounter.

What is sad is the people who stood next to us and believed in the gospel I had shared are no longer going to church at all. My hope is they never let go of the truth they once encountered when Christ laid His life down on the cross for the hope that they might come into relationship with the goodness of their Father. I was happy it did not destroy what God had been doing in my husband's heart for the past three years. Instead of leaving the church altogether, he started attending Ministerio Banderas De Cristo, which is where our first encounter took place. It was where he wanted to be anyway.

We were at that church for three years, all the while working on our little home. I often tell people, my husband and I's relationship was much like the condition of that trailer when we moved in. But with a lot of love, time, and hard work, we completely remolded that trailer, and it was beautiful when we were finished. I had everything in its place and there was a place for everything. We had finally done together what we couldn't do by ourselves and God was in the middle of it all.

In between all of this, my husband remained faithful to his new church. It took some time before I tried going with him. We were there for a couple of years, we had been moved up to the front row, and we attended all the classes. We did our best to be there when it was open and be an active part of the church. When my husband made leadership, I was left behind. Perhaps they felt I was "damaged goods." I am not sure, but I knew I couldn't stay there. I needed something more. I longed to find a church where I felt at home and Tino was okay with letting me try. The truth is, I spent a lot of time trying to jump through hoops that other people created so I would be accepted. I did it all with one hope. The hope that they would let me share, in the church, what Jesus had done for me; I wanted to tell the world of His goodness and how much He loves them. Sometimes, I was told I had a little too much Jesus. I needed to calm it down and take Him out a little at a time, but I couldn't and I didn't want to. I just wanted to find a place I could call home, but mostly I spent my time in woman's conferences and sharing Jesus everywhere I went. I couldn't fit the mold so I made a mold for myself, one that I felt comfortable in while I grew in the knowledge of Him.

Tino went to work and church; he studied for three years and graduated "the Jehova Nissi College," and I opened my own ministry, delivered bread, and shared my testimony wherever I was invited. All the while, we worked on the trailer doing what we could; it was our Father, who worked on our relationship. I remember the day we were offered a bigger trailer on another lot. I had just sat down on the sofa and exhaled. As I looked around our tiny home, I knew I was okay. I thought to myself, "I can do this; it's perfect for us. We have everything we need. There is nothing that we lack."

I had finally become satisfied with what we had. I was basking in the relief I found in being completely content and that is the exact moment the phone rang. The truth was, I hadn't really thought about a bigger place, but God had. He is the one who sees our needs even if we are not paying any mind to them. Truth is, I was minding my own business and there goes God, planning and orchestrating a bigger place for us to move into. Our daughter was three now and I really wanted her to have her own room, something I never had as a child. The neat thing is, I never asked God for it. It was just a silent hope inside my heart. In that moment, I knew He is the Faithful One, who answers even unasked prayers and gives us the desires of our heart.

The amazing thing was the office offered us a trade. They wanted us to exchange our smaller remodeled trailer for the bigger one with two bedrooms and two baths. It definitely came with some sacrifices. It was bigger, but it needed repairs and the lot needed improvements. They also gave me the option to work off the balance by filling in at the office when they needed me. I was on board but my husband was hesitant. We had worked so hard on our little home and had just finished with all the repairs.

It took about three weeks to convince him it was the right move for our family. At first, our neighbors laughed at us and said I hope you have a boat to row yourselves up to the front door. But let me tell you how amazing our God is, they didn't laugh for too long because the day we moved in, my husband's job offered us a load of dirt to raise the land. We were so happy because when it rained the lot flooded and became like a lake. We filled the property, packed the dirt, and realized it wasn't our lot that flooded anymore. Not that we intentionally did that because we didn't, but I guess water has a way of finding the lowest point.

Within the first week, we were offered free pavers in exchange for labor. My husband worked overtime during the weekend and in exchange we got a beautiful new paved driveway. Both of us were amazed at how we watched God move on our behalf. That does not mean we weren't afraid to make the change but we just decided to do it afraid. It scares me to think what we could have lost had we been too afraid to let go of what we had. Just imagine, we could have missed out on understanding the depth of His love, understanding that He sees and knows our needs, our wants, our desires, and is Faithful over it all.

Little did I know, our amazing God had even bigger plans in store for us! By the time we moved into our new trailer and started working on it, our relationship was strengthening. Not only with each other but with God, my husband had done a complete turnaround. He served whole heartedly in his church. We were actually having weekly meetings in our home and sharing the word with people in our neighborhood. I loved to serve up complete meals and fill their bellies before filling their hearts.

While all of these beautiful things were happening, another beautiful thing happened. Our family had grown. God had blessed us with a little guy. We named him Elisha Ryan. Elisha means God is salvation and he was the successor to Elijah in the bible. Ryan is actually considered a Christian boys name and it means little king. It was important to me to name them something that had meaning because they would be called by those meanings for the rest of their life. In my heart his name means he is a successor to the King, a representation of Christ as a little king on earth, a living testament of God's salvation.

It was around that same time that I began to look at houses online. I spent a year looking through real estate. I had no idea how in the world we were going to buy a house. We had no money saved to even afford closing costs. I was not sure if our credit was good enough, but I was about to meet three very important people that would help make it all happen. The first one was a woman who I call "Debbie Christian." She had called me out of the blue and said, "I heard you are interested in buying a house." The truth was, I didn't remember giving out my information but I had asked about a lot of houses. Nonetheless, she informed me she could help. She also lead me to the second person I needed to meet. He was an amazing broker that found a lender to finance our first home. The third person was a very important piece to this amazing puzzle.

She was an older woman. Her daughter had called my office interested in a trailer. It was rare that my husband visited my office, but because it was raining, he stopped by before heading home. When I answered the phone, she asked if there were any trailers for sale. At first I said, "No," my husband said, "Yes, our trailer was for sale for twenty thousand dollars." I gasped, I had no idea we were selling or that we were selling for that much. Nonetheless, before I could stop myself, I repeated those words over the phone. It took a few seconds for them to respond. I was waiting for them to say, "Are you crazy? I'm not paying that kind of money to live in a trailer park." Instead, she said, "Okay, I am on my way to see it now." I sent my husband home to straighten up a bit before she got there. To make a long story short, we sold it that evening.

I was so nervous to tell my boss. After all, I was no longer a fill-in because she had given me a fulltime position. I was so thankful for the opportunities I had received while living in the park and the truth was I thought of her more like a mother than like a boss. Over the years, she had advised me on so many life issues and helped me get through some very difficult times. She had not only been there for me but had provided my family with sustainable income through job security.

I have always looked up to her because of how she carried herself. She is strong but chooses to display her beauty in the meekness of her character. She has the power to be ruthless but more often than not she chooses mercy over justice. She carries herself with grace and wisdom in all that she does, and I appreciate the woman that she is.

I was not nervous because I was scared, I was nervous because her opinion mattered to me. I cared about her input because I respected who she was in my life. It is true she was shocked when I told her. Honestly, I am pretty sure I was in shock to, but I should have known she would be more than happy for our family. After all, she knew the history of us. She has been a firsthand witness to everything we have gone through together.

It took a total of forty-five days to sell our trailer, find a house, close the sale, and move into our new home. As far as I knew, that was a miracle from heaven. I had never heard of anything happening that quickly in the real estate business, but I could be wrong. That is not to say that everything went perfect because there were some obstacles to overcome. We just kept moving forward, one day at a time, until it all worked out, and it worked out quickly.

As soon as we got the keys, we drove to our new address, opened the door, and praised God for His goodness. We sat on the concrete step out back and cried together. We had been through so much. There were so many times we struggled to make ends meet. For a while, we had a twenty-five dollar budget for weekly groceries and he would fish in the river so we could have meat other than hotdogs and bologna. I even had to take our glass penny jar to the grocery store a few times. Once, I can remember praying the entire time that I had enough money to buy our daughters formula. All while asking God to show someone my need and to help me. Instead, what He showed me, was the need of someone else.

I stood in line, holding the jar of money and a can of powdered formula, hoping I had enough. The lady in front of me, who was pregnant, needed twenty-five cents to finish paying for her items. I saw her looking at what she could put back. I knew I had what she needed. I interrupted her and said, "I have it. I have it right here." I dug through the jar and handed over a quarter. I learned one of the greatest lessons of my life that day. I learned that if I would give out of what I had, God would always take care of my needs. I am not sure how that little jar of change did it but I was able to buy formula, bread, milk, and eggs.

I walked out of that grocery store a new person knowing that the God of the universe saw my every need and meet them every single day. The truth is when our cabinets were empty, bags of groceries would show up on our doorstep, and when we had our daughter, she had two baby showers, not one. One was from the Estero church, who loaded us up with everything we could possibly need. They gave us so much that I did not have to buy diapers, wipes, or any other item for six months after her birth. My friend, who we lived with, gave us another shower and another friend, shared with me bags of clothes in all sizes, barely used. We didn't have to buy clothes for a year. I have seen so many miracles and I cannot even begin to fill these pages with all that God has done for us.

When we entered our home, we cried. We cried because we were standing in the middle of our Savior's faithfulness. I knew the house was just a symbol of his goodness but in it held years of learning how to die with Christ so that we could live. In it was the tangible evidence of endurance. The long haul of un-pleasantries and tough situations were finally behind us, and they were behind us because we chose to let Him reign over us. It was here that we stood in ownership with our Savior, never once could we deny His goodness and the mighty works of His hands. His signature was on all of it.

It wasn't the house. It was what the house stood for. It represented the faithfulness of our Savior. We were never out of His reach. He never lost sight of us. He was with us through it all. He had given us His Holy Spirit, who was faithful to teach us in every way, down every path, and never fluttered away at the first sign of difficulty. Instead, all three of them, the Father, the Son, and the Holy Spirit were faithful to stand by us, through thick and thin, never leaving us, nor forsaking us, and here we stand in the middle of our confessions, that He is Lord.

He is Lord over ALL. I had been cast out, turned away, and given up. I had been pressed on every side, but not crushed, perplexed, but not in despair, persecuted, but not abandoned, struck down, but not destroyed (2 Corinthians 4:8). I was standing inside the fortitude of my faith, the finished work of my Savior, and the evidence of His goodness was all around me. He is the one who has blotted out my transgressions. It is Him who states the case of my innocence for I have turned to the Lord who wiped all my tears away and removed all of my sins to be remembered no more. I may not know it all but I know one thing is for sure, I "AM" Forgiven and that…. is Finished.

Chapter Thirteen:
It is Finished

It is Finished! I started my journey broken with nowhere left to turn. I left everything behind and choose to follow Him blindly, not knowing where I was going but trusting His love for me. I went places I did not want to go. I stayed longer in rooms I wanted to run from. I lost hope. I even told God, "I quit," once, but here I am still hanging on the vine with hope I will one day bear the fruit of an amazing Savior. I have been pruned, pricked, uprooted, and replanted, but through it all I am still here.

I am here because there is nothing strong enough to separate me from the Love He gave to me from the cross. There is no height, nor depth, neither angel, nor demon, neither present, nor the future, nor any powers, nor anything else in all creation, will be able to separate me from the love of God that I found in Christ Jesus My Lord (Romans 8:37-39).

It finished the moment Jesus cried out to the Father and gave up His spirit, with those words, the whole world changed, going all the way back to the beginning of time and all the way through until the end. He changed it all by removing the veil between my Father in Heaven and all of creation; the curtain torn for all of eternity, past, present, and future. The world will never again be the same. It is not possible because the yearning for a savior goes deep inside the soul of every single person longing for something more, searching for fulfillment. The empty hole penetrating the heart of every human being has a "one size fits all" answer; salvation in the form of a personal relationship with a savior named Jesus, a Father who loves us, and a teacher, the Holy Spirt, who is not afraid to stay with us through it all.

It is Jesus who laid down His life for all of mankind without conditions. He said, "Come to me all who are weary and heavy laden and I will give you rest" (Matthew 11:28). There was no small print preventing my entrance into His arms. NO circumstances or stipulations that I had to meet before entering into

His Grace. It was His love that found me on that shower floor. It was His love that carried me through the darkest memories and the hardest of times during my journey of learning to know Him more.

The One who came with one purpose, to save the world, and who is He saving the world from? The world is being saved from itself; with its screams of "notice me," "keep me," "protect me," and "me" is exactly the person Jesus saved *me* from. The "ME" that hides inside my soul that hated what I couldn't control, the one that beat, hit, and tortured my mind, the one who allowed fear to dictate every decision and contemplate every response resulting in an endless battle with "self."

The only way I found to get "me" out of the picture was to lay my life down and learn to never pick it back up again. It is the hardest lesson but it is the most valuable. I choose to lay my life down for the King; the only King that could ever fill the black hole that consumed my soul. The only One who could teach me to look outside myself into a hurting and dying world. The One who planted the seed inside of me that I, too, could somehow change the world I was living in. I had, inside of me, the resurrected power to touch the world in a way that only I could.

I was uniquely made, created for His Glory, much like the sun as it sets and rises, creating a unique skyline never to be seen again. It is made new every evening and every morning. The same sky will never be seen twice, for all of eternity, that is how I am made, and that is how you are made. What God has created us for is as unique as His sunsets and sunrises. He is an individual God for us as individuals. I could never have what He has intended for someone else and no one can have what He has intended for me.

It is by His grace through His mercy that I am still here. "I am still." I am no longer fighting. Every moment of every day is another chance to lay my life down for His. He has already paid the price for me to have everything I can dare to hope to imagine.

I have learned to stand on the Word of God in ways that I do not have the ability to express in mere letters written on a page. They aren't sufficient enough to hold the magnitude of what God has done inside of my soul. The truths He has shared with me are like no other. They complete me and make me whole in ways the world could only hope to. There is not one second that I regret, because He has given me value and worth; not the kind that is taken or given by man but the kind that lasts an eternity.

There were some difficult lessons to learn, but they were the most beautiful lessons I could have ever learned. The tears I shed were not because of the pain that people caused me. They were in fact the cleansing tears of repentance. Not the kind that people challenge you with words of condemnation, but a repentance that can only come with the understanding of His love. As a child, I can remember being beaten, yelled at, my little spirit being crushed by the words of childish adults that had no understanding of God's love. In my relationship with my Father in heaven, He has never "beaten me" into submission to Him, He has only loved me to the point that I want to obey Him. Not because He will reward me in some way but because His love is just that kind, it is good, it is gentle, and it is big enough to cover me. It is gentle enough to hold me when I am screaming to let me go. It is good enough to keep me even when I am running away. It is kind enough to cover me and make the best of my mistakes. This is the biggest kind of love ever given and He has given this to me.

When I was child, I talked like a child, I thought like a child, I reasoned like a child, but when I grew up I put my childish ways behind me (1 Corinthians 13:11). I had to learn to be willing to look at myself in every situation. I could no longer look at someone else as the cause of my concern, my life, or any other circumstance I was in. In every situation, I had to be willing to ask God to change me. To make my heart a heart like His. I had to be willing to lay my life down and hand over every issue, trusting that the God of all creation would be faithful to guide me through my tears.

Those tears often came from a revelation that transformed my soul; starting on the inside and working its way out of me. The most painful parts of this journey have been those things in my life that God unveiled from my own eyes, from my own soul, from my own past, and from my own mistakes and decisions.

God never asked me to change anyone else. He never asked me to change myself, but He did promise me that I would be made new each day if I choose Him first. It was my Father who put inside my heart that every moment I choose to give to Him, He will multiply it back to me tenfold. I had to learn that all I do is for my Father and what He desires for me to do. This desire cannot be met by doing what people tell me to do. I had to learn the doors that God opens no man can shut, but the doors "man" opens they can shut. I had to make a decision that even if no one agrees with me, even if the whole world is against me, I will follow the One who Saves.

The only One who gave His life for mine. I had to make a decision in order to live inside the folds of His resurrection; I must also lay down my own life to pick up the "cause" He has given me. To use my gifts for His good pleasure, trusting He will make happen what I cannot. I had to choose to put one foot in front of the other every day, doing the best with what I had for His kingdom. Even though, to me it always seemed so small compared to what was inside my heart.

There are so many times I am reminded of the story of the boy with the lunch and how Jesus fed the multitude out of his few fish and bread (Matthew 14:13-21). Often times, I have felt like all I had was just enough to feed one. What I learn every time I choose to hand over my fish and bread is Jesus is faithful to multiply what I have into something bigger than I can imagine. If I choose to hand over what I have to Him, if I choose to lay my life down for others, if I choose to let Him lead, He will do what I could never do alone.

I am sure, on the day that little boy left his home with just enough for lunch, he had no idea that God chose what He had given to one, to feed the world around him. I believe there is something great in each of us. We all have been equipped with something to "feed" the world around us. To make a difference in the highways and byways we pass on a daily basis. We have a choice to make our lives, where ever we are standing, a pulpit for God's love to reach the people passing by, in the stores, in our jobs, and above all else, those who are in our homes and our families.

What I know today is I can trust Jesus with the little that I have. If all I have is a mustard seed, which is the size of the tip of a pen, to offer to Him, He will be faithful to move mountains from in front of me. If I have a hope for the future, a vision that I cannot let go of, I am positive that Christ can do what I cannot do by myself.

There are mountains in front of us. Sometimes, those mountains look too big to climb, too difficult to master because they come in the form of serving ourselves. It can be difficult to discern the disguise that covers the actions of "servitude" to "self" because they can masquerade in a multitude of colors. Sometimes they are hidden beneath good intentions and clothed by religion in the form of "Christianity." Other times they are lurking under darkness and destruction can be found in the middle of good times and immediate gratification (2 Corinthians 11). Please understand that "I" is always at the center of "self" and it can be difficult for "you" to overcome, but it is not too difficult for Him. Jesus said, "I have told you these things, so that in "Me" you may have peace. In this world you will have trouble. But take heart! I have overcome the world" (John 16:33).

I say all of this to remind you that even if all you have is just a few fish, and a mustard seed of faith, then you have more than enough for Jesus to bring a breakthrough into your life, you have more than enough for Jesus to tear down strongholds inside your mind, you have more than enough to walk with the One who loves you, the One who laid down His life for you. You have more than enough to experience what I have experienced in the last fifteen years of my life. Perhaps the story will alter a bit with details about your own personal journey, but the results will surely be the same because God changes not and He is not a man that He should lie.

Romans 2:11 tells us that God does not show favoritism. What He does for one person He will do for another. His Word tells me that He writes His precepts on my heart and is faithful to lead me. He has called me His sheep and told me I hear His voice and follow Him, and the truth is you have the same hope available to you that I have found in Christ Jesus, the Lord and Savior of my life. Christ was crucified for my cause and yours. There is nothing you will ever do to take away from the cross and there is nothing you will do to add to it. My only hope is that we can learn how to rest in the completed work that only He could accomplish for us.

There is so much to say and so little time. I woke up this morning knowing that I would write today in the hope that it would touch the lives of those who are reading it. The truth is we've all been in that place where we have felt rejected and alone. Places where those who are supposed to love us actually end up hurting us. When I came to the church I was in love with my Jesus. I was in love with the miracle that had taken place on the inside of my soul, and I couldn't wait to become a part of a new family, a family that would embrace me and accept me right where I was. I expected to get a family that was as excited about my Jesus as I was and wanted so badly to share in that excitement. I expected a church to stand by me, to become witnesses to what only God can do, and support my growth and walk in Christ, but I didn't get what I expected.

I learned very quickly, expectations are meant only for the Father. The One who created us in our mother's womb; no one can take

His throne. No, He will not share it. It was not meant for "the church." It was not meant for anyone other than Himself. He has loved us from a-far and once we ask Him in, He will never let us go; He will be there until the very end. No man can stand beneath the pressure of satisfying a position that was meant only for our God. The throne belongs to Him and it is Him who took the throne down from the majesty of the Heavens and placed it inside of our hearts. It is up to each of us to learn the significance of dying to ourselves in order that He may live, that He may continue to walk this earth, and complete the call to save the world.

The Word tells me in John 1:14 "the word became flesh and made his dwelling among us. We have seen his glory, the glory of the one and only Son, who came from the Father, full of grace and truth." The word became the flesh that was Jesus who walked the earth among us and dwelt with us on the same level as every one of us. He physically dwelled here, but Jesus also said in John 14:23 "All who love me will do what I say. My Father will love them, and "We" will come and make our home with each of them." Right there, in this scripture Jesus Himself says He and His Father bring

the throne room down from heaven and place it inside of our hearts

as they both come and dwell with us. In verse twenty-five we can

see He promised us a teacher, the Holy Spirit, who will teach us in

all things, who is our helper and full embodiment of all that He is;

all three in one, living on the inside of us.

In verse twenty-seven Jesus said, "Peace I leave with you, My

peace I give you. I do not give as the world gives. Do not let your

hearts be troubled and do not be afraid." I am here to say there is a

peace that the world offers but it is only temporary and has no

ability to last. That is not the peace Jesus is talking about; He does

not give us a "fleeting peace" like the world. He gives us a peace

that can stand in the middle of any storm; a peace that has the

power to overcome the turmoil in our life and give us

understanding in the middle of our mess.

The truth is, it took a while, I made a lot of mistakes, and there is a good chance I am going to make more, but there is one thing I have learned that can never be taken away from me. I know today, there is nothing I can do that will add to the cross and there is nothing I can do that will ever take away from it. Christ crucified for the hope of the glory that we might come into a full relationship with our Father in Heaven, who created us in His image as unique as every sunrise made for His glory. Created to become One with Him, In Christ, Being forever taught by His Spirit, the very Spirit that is the full embodiment of our Creator and Savior alive and well, living on the inside of each of us.

My only prayer is that we all become One, together in Christ, as He is in the Father and the Father is in Him, so the World may believe that God sent a Savior, a Savior who died to give them life. Who lived to be the perfect demonstration to a dying and hurting world of the Hope that is found in an intimate relationship with a Father whose love is so great that He would send His son to lay His life down to bring us into a full relationship with Himself with the same hope that we may lay our life down for the only hope that saves, redeems, restores, and loves in the purest form ever given to the entire world.

And He did all of that with these three words, "It Is Finished."

So, what have I been doing all these years? I have spent my time getting to know the one who loves me the most and expecting the hope of His Glory to shine brightly through my life. I have been hanging on the vine, being pruned by the "Gardener." What do I mean by that? In John 15 it says, "I am the true vine, and my Father the gardener. He cuts off every branch in me that bears no fruit, while every branch that does bear fruit he prunes so that it will be even more fruitful. You are already clean because of the word I have spoken to you. Remain in me, as I also remain in you. No branch can bear fruit by itself; it must remain on the vine." Jesus has been my vine, when I felt like the whole world was against me, I ran to Him and He was faithful to keep me, to teach me, and to love me right where I was; in the hopes that I may bear much fruit.

I ran to Him through prayer more times than I can count. There were so many nights I begged Him to help me to see and understand the truth. I ran to Him through reading and studying His word and thanking the Holy Spirit for teaching me. I ran to Him when I felt like my world was falling apart and He was faithful to see me through it all. I filled my ears with His truth through listening to proven teachers, prophets, and ministers of all sorts. I protected my eyes from allowing the images of a fallen broken world to invade my soul, to sneak into my heart and deceive me by stealing purity from my soul. I allowed God's truth to change my words, my thoughts, and my actions.

I sought after Him day and night and I still do because He is my life source. He is the one who has all that I need. He has given me a hunger to know what He meant by His final words from the cross, "It is Finished."

I have learned so much by getting to know Him more. Through the intimacy of time spent dwelling in His presence and allowing it to soak into my soul I have learned "it is Finished" means, I cannot out fast Him. I cannot out pray Him. I cannot out live Him, but what I can do is trust that all He has done was done from the cross. I trust in the finished work living on the inside of me. I trust that my Father in Heaven, who loves me, will remove every branch that sucks the life giving love out of me. In other words, I trust He will cut away every part of my heart that is not in line with Him. I trust that He is transforming me into His very own image. An image of my Savior, an image of His love to a hurting and dying world; my only cause is to remain. Remain in His truth, no matter what, until the day my life is over, and my race has come to an end, I will run into His arms, and it will be finally finished.

AFTERWORD

I invite you to the greatest journey of your life. I invite you to join me on the "Something Shiney" journey. I invite you to make it your own and become amazed at a Father who loves you like no other, a Jesus who died to give you everything and come to know a Holy Spirit who will teach you each step of the way. This is the something shinEy journey, a place where God leaves nothing out and makes the ordinary…. extraordinary. Now believe in the prayer that Jesus prayed to his Father when He prayed for us in John 17:20

His Prayer for each of us….

John 17:20

"My prayer is not for them alone. I pray also for those who will believe in me through their message, that all of them may be one, Father, just as you are in me and I am in you, May they also be in us so that the world may believe that you have sent me. I have given them the glory that you gave me, that they may be one as we are one I in them and you in me so that they may be brought to complete unity. Then the world will know that you sent me and have loved them even as you have loved me. Father, I want those you have given me to be with me where I am, and to see my glory, the glory you have given me because you loved me before the creation of the world. Righteous Father, though the world does not know you I know you and they know that you have sent me. I have made you known to them, and will continue to make you known in order that the love you have for me may be in them and that I myself may be in them"....

I invite you to come and see what God is doing for yourself,

Give God a Chance, and

Accept Jesus into your Heart by saying,

I believe you are the Son of God, I believe you gave your life for me, so that I would be saved from my sins every day and come into knowing what it is like to have a personal relationship with my Father in Heaven who loves me.

Thank you Jesus!

I receive into my heart the promised gift of the Holy Spirit to come and dwell inside me, to teach and to guide me all the days of my life. I ask that You let my life become a letter of Your Grace and Your Mercy sharing in the only Glory that comes from knowing a Savior like You!

Thank you Father, Thank you Jesus, and Thank you Holy Spirit!

Now from this day forward I want you to understand one thing. The work that Jesus has done is finished in you. There is nothing you can do that will take away from the cross and there is nothing you are going to do to add to it. It is your job to know for yourself what it is that Jesus did when He said, It Is Finished!

Because the Truth is

It Is Finished!

FROM THE AUTHOR

I want you all to know how much I appreciate you taking the time to read my story. According to "popular belief" no one wants to read a memoir from a no-name un-famous no-body from nowhere. So I want to say Thank You! You mean the world to me.

My desire is to be part of a solution and to stop the suffering before it starts. I am determined to use my life and my experiences to bring comfort to the brokenhearted and so, I am asking you to join me in these efforts by sharing my book with someone in your life.

Thank you Again and I leave you with this thought, "if one person can put a thousand to flight and two, ten thousand, just imagine what we could do together.

My prayer is and forever will be that each one of us be the church in our everyday lives because we are "the church."

Made in the USA
Columbia, SC
24 October 2020

23277013R00207